# HISTORY & GEOGRAPHY 600
## Teacher's Guide

W9-CMZ-846

**Author:**

Alpha Omega Publications

**Editor:**

Alan Christopherson, M.S.

**804 N. 2nd Ave. E.**
**Rock Rapids, IA 51246-1759**

# HISTORY & GEOGRAPHY 600

LIFEPAC® Overview

# HISTORY & GEOGRAPHY SCOPE & SEQUENCE

| | Grade 1 | Grade 2 | Grade 3 |
|---|---|---|---|
| UNIT 1 | I AM A SPECIAL PERSON<br>• God made me<br>• All about you<br>• Using proper manners | FAMILIES AND NEIGHBORS<br>• We need a family<br>• We help our family<br>• Our neighborhood<br>• Helping our neighbors | U.S. GEOGRAPHY AND HISTORY STUDY SKILLS<br>• Map skills<br>• Resources<br>• Community |
| UNIT 2 | COMMUNICATING WITH SOUND<br>• Sounds people make<br>• Sounds that communicate<br>• Communicating without sound<br>• Communicating with God | COMMUNITY HELPERS<br>• What is a community<br>• Community helpers<br>• Your church community<br>• Helping your community | NEW ENGLAND STATES<br>• ME, NH, VT, MA, RI, AND CT<br>• New England geography<br>• New England resources<br>• New England community |
| UNIT 3 | I HAVE FEELINGS<br>• I feel sad<br>• I feel afraid<br>• I feel happy<br>• I have other feelings | NEIGHBORHOOD STORES<br>• Pioneer goods and services<br>• Modern goods and services<br>• Some business rules<br>• God's business rules | MID-ATLANTIC STATES<br>• NY, PA, NJ, DE, MD, and DC<br>• Mid-Atlantic geography<br>• Mid-Atlantic resources<br>• Mid-Atlantic community |
| UNIT 4 | I LIVE IN A FAMILY<br>• My mother and father<br>• My brothers and sisters<br>• My grandparents<br>• What my family does | FARMS AND CITIES<br>• Farming long ago<br>• Farming today<br>• Growing cities<br>• Changing cities | SOUTHERN ATLANTIC STATES<br>• WV, VA, NC, SC, GA, AND FL<br>• Southern Atlantic geography<br>• Southern Atlantic resources<br>• Southern Atlantic community |
| UNIT 5 | YOU AND GOD'S FAMILY<br>• Getting ready in the morning<br>• Walking to school<br>• The school family<br>• The church family | NEIGHBORS AROUND THE WORLD<br>• Things all families need<br>• How communities share<br>• How communities change<br>• Customs of the world | SOUTHERN STATES<br>• KY, TN, MS, LA, AL, OK, TX, AND AR<br>• Southern geography<br>• Southern resources<br>• Southern community |
| UNIT 6 | PLACES PEOPLE LIVE<br>• Life on the farm<br>• Life in the city<br>• Life by the sea | A JAPANESE FAMILY<br>• Places people live in Japan<br>• School in Japan<br>• Work in Japan<br>• Play in Japan | GREAT LAKES STATES<br>• OH, IN, IL, MI, WI, and MN<br>• Great Lakes geography<br>• Great Lakes resources<br>• Great Lakes community |
| UNIT 7 | COMMUNITY HELPERS<br>• Firemen and policemen<br>• Doctors<br>• City workers<br>• Teachers and ministers | HOW WE TRAVEL<br>• Travel in Bible times<br>• Travel in the past<br>• Travel today<br>• Silent consonants • Homonyms | MIDWESTERN STATES<br>• ND, SD, NE, KS, MO, and IA<br>• Midwestern geography<br>• Midwestern resources<br>• Midwestern community |
| UNIT 8 | I LOVE MY COUNTRY<br>• America discovered<br>• The Pilgrims<br>• The United States begin<br>• Respect for your country | MESSAGES FROM FAR AND NEAR<br>• Communication in Bible times<br>• Communication today<br>• Reasons for communication<br>• Communication without sound | MOUNTAIN STATES<br>• MT, ID, WY, NV, UT, CO, AZ, and NM<br>• Mountain geography<br>• Mountain resources<br>• Mountain community |
| UNIT 9 | I LIVE IN THE WORLD<br>• The globe<br>• Countries<br>• Friends in Mexico<br>• Friends in Japan | CARING FOR OUR NEIGHBORHOODS<br>• God's plan for nature<br>• Sin changed nature<br>• Problems in our neighborhoods<br>• Helping our neighborhoods | PACIFIC STATES<br>• WA, OR, CA, AK, and HI<br>• Pacific geography<br>• Pacific resources<br>• Pacific community |
| UNIT 10 | THE WORLD AND YOU<br>• You are special<br>• Your family<br>• Your school and church<br>• Your world | PEOPLE DEPEND ON EACH OTHER<br>• Depending on our families<br>• Depending on our neighbors<br>• Depending on our communities<br>• Communicating with God | U.S. GEOGRAPHY AND HISTORY REVIEW<br>• U.S. geographical features<br>• Eastern U.S. review<br>• Western U.S. review |

# HISTORY & GEOGRAPHY SCOPE & SEQUENCE

| Grade 4 | Grade 5 | Grade 6 | |
|---|---|---|---|
| OUR EARTH<br>• The surface of the earth<br>• Early explorations of the earth<br>• Exploring from space<br>• Exploring the oceans | A NEW WORLD<br>• Exploration of America<br>• The first colonies<br>• Conflict with Britain<br>• Birth of the United States | WORLD GEOGRAPHY<br>• Latitude and longitude<br>• Western and eastern hemispheres<br>• The southern hemisphere<br>• Political and cultural regions | UNIT 1 |
| SEAPORT CITIES<br>• Sydney<br>• Hong Kong<br>• Istanbul<br>• London | A NEW NATION<br>• War for Independence<br>• Life in America<br>• A new form of government<br>• The Nation's early years | THE CRADLE OF CIVILIZATION<br>• Mesopotamia<br>• The land of Israel<br>• The Nation of Israel<br>• Egypt | UNIT 2 |
| DESERT LANDS<br>• What is a desert?<br>• Where are the deserts?<br>• How do people live in the desert? | A TIME OF TESTING<br>• Louisiana Purchase<br>• War of 1812<br>• Sectionalism<br>• Improvements in trade & travel | GREECE AND ROME<br>• Geography of the region<br>• Beginning civilizations<br>• Contributions to other civilizations<br>• The influence of Christianity | UNIT 3 |
| GRASSLANDS<br>• Grasslands of the world<br>• Ukraine<br>• Kenya<br>• Argentina | A GROWING NATION<br>• Andrew Jackson's influence<br>• Texas & Oregon<br>• Mexican War<br>• The Nation divides | THE MIDDLE AGES<br>• The feudal system<br>• Books and schools<br>• The Crusades<br>• Trade and architecture | UNIT 4 |
| TROPICAL RAIN FORESTS<br>• Facts about rain forests<br>• Rain forests of the world<br>• The Amazon rain forest<br>• The Congo rain forest | A DIVIDED NATION<br>• Civil War<br>• Reconstruction<br>• Gilded Age<br>• The need for reform | SIX SOUTH AMERICAN COUNTRIES<br>• Brazil<br>• Colombia<br>• Venezuela<br>• Three Guianas | UNIT 5 |
| THE POLAR REGIONS<br>• The polar regions: coldest places in the world<br>• The Arctic polar region<br>• The Antarctic polar region | A CHANGING NATION<br>• Progressive reforms<br>• Spanish-American War<br>• World War I<br>• Roaring Twenties | OTHER AMERICAN COUNTRIES<br>• Ecuador and Peru<br>• Bolivia and Uruguay<br>• Paraguay and Argentina<br>• Chile | UNIT 6 |
| MOUNTAIN COUNTRIES<br>• Peru – the Andes<br>• The Incas and modern Peru<br>• Nepal – the Himalayas<br>• Switzerland – the Alps | DEPRESSION AND WAR<br>• The Great Depression<br>• War begins in Europe<br>• War in Europe<br>• War in the Pacific | AFRICA<br>• Geography and cultures<br>• Countries of northern Africa<br>• Countries of central Africa<br>• Countries of southern Africa | UNIT 7 |
| ISLAND COUNTRIES<br>• Islands of the earth<br>• Cuba<br>• Iceland<br>• Japan | COLD WAR<br>• Korean War & other crises<br>• Vietnam War<br>• Civil Rights Movement<br>• Upheaval in America | MODERN WESTERN EUROPE<br>• The Renaissance<br>• The Industrial Revolution<br>• World War I<br>• World War II | UNIT 8 |
| NORTH AMERICA<br>• Geography<br>• Lands, lakes and rivers<br>• Northern countries<br>• Southern countries | INTO THE NEW MILLENNIUM<br>• Watergate and détente<br>• The fall of Communism<br>• The Persian Gulf<br>• Issues of the new millennium | MODERN EASTERN EUROPE<br>• Early government<br>• Early churches<br>• Early countries<br>• Modern countries | UNIT 9 |
| OUR WORLD IN REVIEW<br>• Europe and the explorers<br>• Asia and Africa<br>• Southern continents<br>• North America, North Pole | THE UNITED STATES OF AMERICA<br>• Beginning America until 1830<br>• Stronger America 1830-1930<br>• 1930 to the end of the millennium<br>• The new millennium | THE DEVELOPMENT OF OUR WORLD<br>• Cradle of civilization<br>• The Middle Ages<br>• Modern Europe<br>• South America and Africa | UNIT 10 |

# HISTORY & GEOGRAPHY SCOPE & SEQUENCE

| | Grade 7 | Grade 8 | Grade 9 |
|---|---|---|---|
| **UNIT 1** | **WHAT IS HISTORY**<br>• Definition and significance of history<br>• Historians and the historical method<br>• Writing an outline<br>• Views of history | **EUROPE COMES TO AMERICA**<br>• Voyages of Columbus<br>• Spanish exploration<br>• Other exploration<br>• The first colonies | **UNITED STATES HERITAGE**<br>• American colonies<br>• Acquisitions and annexations<br>• Backgrounds to freedom<br>• Backgrounds to society |
| **UNIT 2** | **WHAT IS GEOGRAPHY**<br>• Classes of geography<br>• Geography and relief of the earth<br>• Maps and the study of our world<br>• Time zones | **BRITISH AMERICA**<br>• English colonies<br>• Government<br>• Lifestyle<br>• Wars with France | **OUR NATIONAL GOVERNMENT**<br>• Ideals of national government<br>• National government developed<br>• Legislative and Executive branches<br>• Judicial branch |
| **UNIT 3** | **U.S. HISTORY AND GEOGRAPHY**<br>• Geography of the U.S.<br>• Early history of the U.S.<br>• Physical regions of the U.S.<br>• Cultural regions of the U.S. | **THE AMERICAN REVOLUTION**<br>• British control<br>• Rebellion of the Colonies<br>• War for Independence<br>• Constitution | **STATE AND LOCAL GOVERNMENT**<br>• Powers of state government<br>• County government<br>• Township government<br>• City government |
| **UNIT 4** | **ANTHROPOLOGY**<br>• Understanding anthropology<br>• The unity of man<br>• The diversity of man<br>• The culture of man | **A FIRM FOUNDATION**<br>• Washington's presidency<br>• Adams administration<br>• Jeffersonian Democracy<br>• War of 1812 | **PLANNING A CAREER**<br>• Definition of a career<br>• God's will concerning a career<br>• Selecting a career<br>• Preparation for a career |
| **UNIT 5** | **SOCIOLOGY**<br>• Sociology defined<br>• Historical development<br>• Importance to Christians<br>• Method of sociology | **A GROWING NATION**<br>• Jacksonian Era<br>• Northern border<br>• Southern border<br>• Industrial Revolution | **CITIZENSHIP**<br>• Citizenship defined<br>• Gaining citizenship<br>• Rights of citizenship<br>• Responsibilities of citizenship |
| **UNIT 6** | **U.S. ANTHROPOLOGY**<br>• Cultural background of the U.S.<br>• Native American cultures<br>• Cultures from distant lands<br>• Cultural and social interaction | **THE CIVIL WAR**<br>• Division & Secession<br>• Civil War<br>• Death of Lincoln<br>• Reconstruction | **THE EARTH AND MAN**<br>• Man inhabits the earth<br>• Man's home on the earth<br>• Man develops the earth<br>• The future of the earth |
| **UNIT 7** | **ECONOMICS**<br>• Economics defined<br>• Methods of the economist<br>• Tools of the economist<br>• An experiment in economy | **GILDED AGE TO PROGRESSIVE ERA**<br>• Rise of industry<br>• Wild West<br>• America as a world power<br>• Progressive era | **REGIONS OF THE WORLD**<br>• A region defined<br>• Geographic and climate regions<br>• Cultural and political regions<br>• Economic regions of Europe |
| **UNIT 8** | **POLITICAL SCIENCE**<br>• Definition of political science<br>• Roots of Western thought<br>• Modern political thinkers<br>• Political theory | **A WORLD IN CONFLICT**<br>• World War I<br>• Great Depression<br>• New Deal<br>• World War II | **MAN AND HIS ENVIRONMENT**<br>• The physical environment<br>• Drug abuse<br>• The social environment<br>• Man's responsibilities |
| **UNIT 9** | **STATE ECONOMICS AND POLITICS**<br>• Background of state government<br>• State government<br>• State finance<br>• State politics | **COLD WAR AMERICA**<br>• Origins of the Cold War<br>• Vietnam<br>• Truman to Nixon<br>• Ending of the Cold War | **TOOLS OF THE GEOGRAPHER**<br>• The globe<br>• Types of maps<br>• Reading maps<br>• The earth in symbol form |
| **UNIT 10** | **SOCIAL SCIENCES REVIEW**<br>• History and geography<br>• Anthropology<br>• Sociology<br>• Economics and politics | **RECENT AMERICA & REVIEW**<br>• Europe to Independence<br>• Colonies to the Civil War<br>• Civil War to World War II<br>• World War II through Cold War | **MAN IN A CHANGING WORLD**<br>• Development of the nation<br>• Development of government<br>• Development of the earth<br>• Solving problems |

# HISTORY & GEOGRAPHY SCOPE & SEQUENCE

| Grade 10 | Grade 11 | Grade 12 | |
|---|---|---|---|
| ANCIENT CIVILIZATION<br>• Origin of civilization<br>• Early Egypt<br>• Assyria and Babylonia<br>• Persian civilization | FOUNDATIONS OF DEMOCRACY<br>• Democracy develops<br>• Virginia<br>• New England colonies<br>• Middle and southern colonies | INTERNATIONAL GOVERNMENTS<br>• Why have governments<br>• Types of governments<br>• Governments in our world<br>• Political thinkers | UNIT 1 |
| ANCIENT CIVILIZATIONS<br>• India<br>• China<br>• Greek civilization<br>• Roman Empire | CONSTITUTIONAL GOVERNMENT<br>• Relations with England<br>• The Revolutionary War<br>• Articles of Confederation<br>• Constitution of the U.S. | UNITED STATES GOVERNMENT<br>• U.S. Constitution<br>• Bill of Rights<br>• Three branches of government<br>• Legislative process | UNIT 2 |
| THE MEDIEVAL WORLD<br>• Early Middle Ages<br>• Middle Ages in transition<br>• High Middle Ages | NATIONAL EXPANSION<br>• A strong federal government<br>• Revolution of 1800<br>• War of 1812<br>• Nationalism and sectionalism | AMERICAN PARTY SYSTEM<br>• American party system<br>• Development of political parties<br>• Functions of political parties<br>• Voting | UNIT 3 |
| RENAISSANCE AND REFORMATION<br>• Changes in government and art<br>• Changes in literature and thought<br>• Advances in science<br>• Reform within the Church | A NATION DIVIDED<br>• Issues of division<br>• Division of land and people<br>• Economics of slavery<br>• Politics of slavery | HISTORY OF GOVERNMENTS<br>• Primitive governments<br>• Beginnings of Democracy<br>• Feudalism, Theocracy & Democracy<br>• Fascism & Nazism | UNIT 4 |
| GROWTH OF WORLD EMPIRES<br>• England and France<br>• Portugal and Spain<br>• Austria and Germany<br>• Italy and the Ottoman Empire | A NATION UNITED AGAIN<br>• Regionalism<br>• The Division<br>• The Civil War<br>• Reconstruction | THE CHRISTIAN & GOVERNMENT<br>• Discrimination & the Christian<br>• Christian attitudes<br>• "Opinion & Truth" in politics<br>• Politics & Propaganda | UNIT 5 |
| THE AGE OF REVOLUTION<br>• Factors leading to revolution<br>• The English Revolution<br>• The American Revolution<br>• The French Revolution | INVOLVEMENT AT HOME & ABROAD<br>• Surge of industry<br>• The industrial lifestyle<br>• Isolationism<br>• Involvement in conflict | FREE ENTERPRISE<br>• Economics<br>• Competition<br>• Money through history<br>• International finance & currency | UNIT 6 |
| THE INDUSTRIAL REVOLUTION<br>• Sparks of preparation<br>• Industrial revolution in England<br>• Industrial revolution in America<br>• Social changes of the revolution | THE SEARCH FOR PEACE<br>• The War and its aftermath<br>• The Golden Twenties<br>• The Great Depression<br>• The New Deal | BUSINESS AND YOU<br>• Running a business<br>• Government & Business<br>• Banks & Mergers<br>• Deregulation & Bankruptcy | UNIT 7 |
| TWO WORLD WARS<br>• Mounting tension<br>• World War I<br>• Peace and power quests<br>• World War II | A NATION AT WAR<br>• Causes of the war<br>• World War II<br>• Korean Conflict<br>• Vietnam Conflict | THE STOCK MARKET<br>• How it started and works<br>• Selecting stocks<br>• Types of stocks<br>• Tracking stocks | UNIT 8 |
| THE CONTEMPORARY WORLD<br>• The Cold War<br>• Korean War and Vietnam War<br>• Collapse of the Soviet Union<br>• Today's world | CONTEMPORARY AMERICA<br>• America in the 1960s<br>• America in the 1970s<br>• America in the 80s & 90s<br>• International Scene 1980-Present | BUDGET AND FINANCE<br>• Cash, Credit & Checking<br>• Buying a car<br>• Grants, Loans & IRAs<br>• Savings & E-cash | UNIT 9 |
| ANCIENT TIMES TO THE PRESENT<br>• Ancient civilizations<br>• Medieval times<br>• The Renaissance<br>• The modern world | UNITED STATES HISTORY<br>• Basis of democracy<br>• The 1800s<br>• Industrialization<br>• Current history | GEOGRAPHY AND REVIEW<br>• Euro & International finance<br>• U.S. Geography<br>• The global traveler<br>• Neighbors, Heroes & The Holy Land | UNIT 10 |

# STRUCTURE OF THE LIFEPAC CURRICULUM

The LIFEPAC curriculum is conveniently structured to provide one teacher handbook containing teacher support material with answer keys and ten student worktexts for each subject at grade levels two through twelve. The worktext format of the LIFEPACs allows the student to read the textual information and complete workbook activities all in the same booklet. The easy to follow LIFEPAC numbering system lists the grade as the first number(s) and the last two digits as the number of the series. For example, the Language Arts LIFEPAC at the 6th grade level, 5th book in the series would be LAN0605.

Each LIFEPAC is divided into 3 to 5 sections and begins with an introduction or overview of the booklet as well as a series of specific learning objectives to give a purpose to the study of the LIFEPAC. The introduction and objectives are followed by a vocabulary section which may be found at the beginning of each section at the lower levels, at the beginning of the LIFEPAC in the middle grades, or in the glossary at the high school level. Vocabulary words are used to develop word recognition and should not be confused with the spelling words introduced later in the LIFEPAC. The student should learn all vocabulary words before working the LIFEPAC sections to improve comprehension, retention, and reading skills.

Each activity or written assignment has a number for easy identification, such as 1.1. The first number corresponds to the LIFEPAC section and the number to the right of the decimal is the number of the activity.

Teacher checkpoints, which are essential to maintain quality learning, are found at various locations throughout the LIFEPAC. The teacher should check 1) neatness of work and penmanship, 2) quality of understanding (tested with a short oral quiz), 3) thoroughness of answers (complete sentences and paragraphs, correct spelling, etc.), 4) completion of activities (no blank spaces), and 5) accuracy of answers as compared to the answer key (all answers correct).

The self test questions are also number coded for easy reference. For example, 2.015 means that this is the 15th question in the self test of Section 2. The first number corresponds to the LIFEPAC section, the zero indicates that it is a self test question, and the number to the right of the zero the question number.

The LIFEPAC test is packaged at the centerfold of each LIFEPAC. It should be removed and put aside before giving the booklet to the student for study.

Answer and test keys have the same numbering system as the LIFEPACs. The student may be given access to the answer keys (not the test keys) under teacher supervision so that he can score his own work.

A thorough study of the Curriculum Overview by the teacher before instruction begins is essential to the success of the student. The teacher should become familiar with expected skill mastery and understand how these grade level skills fit into the overall skill development of the curriculum. The teacher should also preview the objectives that appear at the beginning of each LIFEPAC for additional preparation and planning.

# TEST SCORING AND GRADING

Answer keys and test keys give examples of correct answers. They convey the idea, but the student may use many ways to express a correct answer. The teacher should check for the essence of the answer, not for the exact wording. Many questions are high level and require thinking and creativity on the part of the student. Each answer should be scored based on whether or not the main idea written by the student matches the model example. "Any Order" or "Either Order" in a key indicates that no particular order is necessary to be correct.

Most self tests and LIFEPAC tests at the lower elementary levels are scored at 1 point per answer; however, the upper levels may have a point system awarding 2 to 5 points for various answers or questions. Further, the total test points will vary; they may not always equal 100 points. They may be 78, 85, 100, 105, etc.

**Example 1**

**Example 2**

A score box similar to ex. 1 above is located at the end of each self test and on the front of the LIFEPAC test. The bottom score, 72, represents the total number of points possible on the test. The upper score, 58, represents the number of points your student will need to receive an 80% or passing grade. If you wish to establish the exact percentage that your student has achieved, find the total points of his correct answers and divide it by the bottom number (in this case 72.) For example, if your student has a point total of 65, divide 65 by 72 for a grade of 90%. Referring to ex. 2, on a test with a total of 105 possible points, the student would have to receive a minimum of 84 correct points for an 80% or passing grade. If your student has received 93 points, simply divide the 93 by 105 for a percentage grade of 89%. Students who receive a score below 80% should review the LIFEPAC and retest using the appropriate Alternate Test found in the Teacher's Guide.

The following is a guideline to assign letter grades for completed LIFEPACs based on a maximum total score of 100 points.

**Example:**

| | | |
|---|---|---|
| LIFEPAC Test | = | 60% of the Total Score (or percent grade) |
| Self Test | = | 25% of the Total Score (average percent of self tests) |
| Reports | = | 10% or 10* points per LIFEPAC |
| Oral Work | = | 5% or 5* points per LIFEPAC |

*Determined by the teacher's subjective evaluation of the student's daily work.

**Example:**

| | | | | | |
|---|---|---|---|---|---|
| LIFEPAC Test Score | = | 92% | 92 x .60 | = | 55 points |
| Self Test Average | = | 90% | 90 x .25 | = | 23 points |
| Reports | | | | = | 8 points |
| Oral Work | | | | = | 4 points |

| | | |
|---|---|---|
| TOTAL POINTS | = | 90 points |

**Grade Scale based on point system:**

| | | |
|---|---|---|
| 100 – 94 | = | A |
| 93 – 86 | = | B |
| 85 – 77 | = | C |
| 76 – 70 | = | D |
| Below 70 | = | F |

# TEACHER HINTS AND STUDYING TECHNIQUES

LIFEPAC Activities are written to check the level of understanding of the preceding text. The student may look back to the text as necessary to complete these activities; however, a student should never attempt to do the activities without reading (studying) the text first. Self tests and LIFEPAC tests are never open book tests.

Language arts activities (skill integration) often appear within other subject curriculum. The purpose is to give the student an opportunity to test his skill mastery outside of the context in which it was presented.

Writing complete answers (paragraphs) to some questions is an integral part of the LIFEPAC Curriculum in all subjects. This builds communication and organization skills, increases understanding and retention of ideas, and helps enforce good penmanship. Complete sentences should be encouraged for this type of activity. Obviously, single words or phrases do not meet the intent of the activity, since multiple lines are given for the response.

Review is essential to student success. Time invested in review where review is suggested will be time saved in correcting errors later. Self tests, unlike the section activities, are closed book. This procedure helps to identify weaknesses before they become too great to overcome. Certain objectives from self tests are cumulative and test previous sections; therefore, good preparation for a self test must include all material studied up to that testing point.

The following procedure checklist has been found to be successful in developing good study habits in the LIFEPAC curriculum.

1. Read the introduction and Table of Contents.
2. Read the objectives.
3. Recite and study the entire vocabulary (glossary) list.
4. Study each section as follows:
   a. Read the introduction and study the section objectives.
   b. Read all the text for the entire section, but answer none of the activities.
   c. Return to the beginning of the section and memorize each vocabulary word and definition.
   d. Reread the section, complete the activities, check the answers with the answer key, correct all errors, and have the teacher check.
   e. Read the self test but do not answer the questions.
   f. Go to the beginning of the first section and reread the text and answers to the activities up to the self test you have not yet done.
   g. Answer the questions to the self test without looking back.
   h. Have the self test checked by the teacher.
   i. Correct the self test and have the teacher check the corrections.
   j. Repeat steps a–i for each section.
5. Use the SQ3R method to prepare for the LIFEPAC test.
   **S**can the whole LIFEPAC.
   **Q**uestion yourself on the objectives.
   **R**ead the whole LIFEPAC again.
   **R**ecite through an oral examination.
   **R**eview weak areas
6. Take the LIFEPAC test as a closed book test.
7. LIFEPAC tests are administered and scored under direct teacher supervision. Students who receive scores below 80% should review the LIFEPAC using the SQ3R study method and take the Alternate Test located in the Teacher Handbook. The final test grade may be the grade on the Alternate Test or an average of the grades from the original LIFEPAC test and the Alternate Test.

# GOAL SETTING AND SCHEDULES

Each school must develop its own schedule, because no single set of procedures will fit every situation. The following is an example of a daily schedule that includes the five LIFEPAC subjects as well as time slotted for special activities.

**Possible Daily Schedule**

| | | |
|---|---|---|
| 8:15 – 8:25 | Pledges, prayer, songs, devotions, etc. |
| 8:25 – 9:10 | Bible |
| 9:10 – 9:55 | Language Arts |
| 9:55 – 10:15 | Recess (juice break) |
| 10:15 – 11:00 | Math |
| 11:00 – 11:45 | History & Geography |
| 11:45 – 12:30 | Lunch, recess, quiet time |
| 12:30 – 1:15 | Science |
| 1:15 – | Drill, remedial work, enrichment* |

*__Enrichment:__ *Computer time, physical education, field trips, fun reading, games and puzzles, family business, hobbies, resource persons, guests, crafts, creative work, electives, music appreciation, projects.*

Basically, two factors need to be considered when assigning work to a student in the LIFEPAC curriculum.

The first is time. An average of 45 minutes should be devoted to each subject, each day. Remember, this is only an average. Because of extenuating circumstances a student may spend only 15 minutes on a subject one day and the next day spend 90 minutes on the same subject.

The second factor is the number of pages to be worked in each subject. A single LIFEPAC is designed to take 3 to 4 weeks to complete. Allowing about 3-4 days for LIFEPAC introduction, review, and tests, the student has approximately 15 days to complete the LIFEPAC pages. Simply take the number of pages in the LIFEPAC, divide it by 15 and you will have the number of pages that must be completed on a daily basis to keep the student on schedule. For example, a LIFEPAC containing 45 pages will require 3 completed pages per day. Again, this is only an average. While working a 45 page LIFEPAC, the student may complete only 1 page the first day if the text has a lot of activities or reports, but go on to complete 5 pages the next day.

Long range planning requires some organization. Because the traditional school year originates in the early fall of one year and continues to late spring of the following year, a calendar should be devised that covers this period of time. Approximate beginning and completion dates can be noted on the calendar as well as special occasions such as holidays, vacations and birthdays. Since each LIFEPAC takes 3-4 weeks or eighteen days to complete, it should take about 180 school days to finish a set of ten LIFEPACs. Starting at the beginning school date, mark off eighteen school days on the calendar and that will become the targeted completion date for the first LIFEPAC. Continue marking the calendar until you have established dates for the remaining nine LIFEPACs making adjustments for previously noted holidays and vacations. If all five subjects are being used, the ten established target dates should be the same for the LIFEPACs in each subject.

# TEACHING SUPPLEMENTS

The sample weekly lesson plan and student grading sheet forms are included in this section as teacher support materials and may be duplicated at the convenience of the teacher.

The student grading sheet is provided for those who desire to follow the suggested guidelines for assignment of letter grades as previously discussed. The student's self test scores should be posted as percentage grades. When the LIFEPAC is completed the teacher should average the self test grades, multiply the average by .25 and post the points in the box marked self test points. The LIFEPAC percentage grade should be multiplied by .60 and posted. Next, the teacher should award and post points for written reports and oral work. A report may be any type of written work assigned to the student whether it is a LIFEPAC or additional learning activity. Oral work includes the student's ability to respond orally to questions which may or may not be related to LIFEPAC activities or any type of oral report assigned by the teacher. The points may then be totaled and a final grade entered along with the date that the LIFEPAC was completed.

The Student Record Book, which was specifically designed for use with the Alpha Omega curriculum, provides space to record weekly progress for one student over a nine week period as well as a place to post self test and LIFEPAC scores. The Student Record Books are available through the current Alpha Omega catalog; however, unlike the enclosed forms these books are not for duplication and should be purchased in sets of four to cover a full academic year.

## WEEKLY LESSON PLANNER

Week of:

| | Subject | Subject | Subject | Subject |
|---|---|---|---|---|
| **Monday** | | | | |
| **Tuesday** | | | | |
| **Wednesday** | | | | |
| **Thursday** | | | | |
| **Friday** | | | | |

## WEEKLY LESSON PLANNER

Week of:

|  | Subject | Subject | Subject | Subject |
|---|---|---|---|---|
| **Monday** | | | | |
| **Tuesday** | | | | |
| **Wednesday** | | | | |
| **Thursday** | | | | |
| **Friday** | | | | |

Student Name _____     Year _____

## Bible

| LP # | Self Test Scores by Sections 1 | 2 | 3 | 4 | 5 | Self Test Points | LIFEPAC Test | Oral Points | Report Points | Final Grade | Date |
|------|---|---|---|---|---|---|---|---|---|---|---|
| 01 | | | | | | | | | | | |
| 02 | | | | | | | | | | | |
| 03 | | | | | | | | | | | |
| 04 | | | | | | | | | | | |
| 05 | | | | | | | | | | | |
| 06 | | | | | | | | | | | |
| 07 | | | | | | | | | | | |
| 08 | | | | | | | | | | | |
| 09 | | | | | | | | | | | |
| 10 | | | | | | | | | | | |

## History & Geography

| LP # | Self Test Scores by Sections 1 | 2 | 3 | 4 | 5 | Self Test Points | LIFEPAC Test | Oral Points | Report Points | Final Grade | Date |
|------|---|---|---|---|---|---|---|---|---|---|---|
| 01 | | | | | | | | | | | |
| 02 | | | | | | | | | | | |
| 03 | | | | | | | | | | | |
| 04 | | | | | | | | | | | |
| 05 | | | | | | | | | | | |
| 06 | | | | | | | | | | | |
| 07 | | | | | | | | | | | |
| 08 | | | | | | | | | | | |
| 09 | | | | | | | | | | | |
| 10 | | | | | | | | | | | |

## Language Arts

| LP # | Self Test Scores by Sections 1 | 2 | 3 | 4 | 5 | Self Test Points | LIFEPAC Test | Oral Points | Report Points | Final Grade | Date |
|------|---|---|---|---|---|---|---|---|---|---|---|
| 01 | | | | | | | | | | | |
| 02 | | | | | | | | | | | |
| 03 | | | | | | | | | | | |
| 04 | | | | | | | | | | | |
| 05 | | | | | | | | | | | |
| 06 | | | | | | | | | | | |
| 07 | | | | | | | | | | | |
| 08 | | | | | | | | | | | |
| 09 | | | | | | | | | | | |
| 10 | | | | | | | | | | | |

Student Name _____    Year _____

## Mathematics

| LP # | Self Test Scores by Sections 1 | 2 | 3 | 4 | 5 | Self Test Points | LIFEPAC Test | Oral Points | Report Points | Final Grade | Date |
|---|---|---|---|---|---|---|---|---|---|---|---|
| 01 | | | | | | | | | | | |
| 02 | | | | | | | | | | | |
| 03 | | | | | | | | | | | |
| 04 | | | | | | | | | | | |
| 05 | | | | | | | | | | | |
| 06 | | | | | | | | | | | |
| 07 | | | | | | | | | | | |
| 08 | | | | | | | | | | | |
| 09 | | | | | | | | | | | |
| 10 | | | | | | | | | | | |

## Science

| LP # | Self Test Scores by Sections 1 | 2 | 3 | 4 | 5 | Self Test Points | LIFEPAC Test | Oral Points | Report Points | Final Grade | Date |
|---|---|---|---|---|---|---|---|---|---|---|---|
| 01 | | | | | | | | | | | |
| 02 | | | | | | | | | | | |
| 03 | | | | | | | | | | | |
| 04 | | | | | | | | | | | |
| 05 | | | | | | | | | | | |
| 06 | | | | | | | | | | | |
| 07 | | | | | | | | | | | |
| 08 | | | | | | | | | | | |
| 09 | | | | | | | | | | | |
| 10 | | | | | | | | | | | |

## Spelling/Electives

| LP # | Self Test Scores by Sections 1 | 2 | 3 | 4 | 5 | Self Test Points | LIFEPAC Test | Oral Points | Report Points | Final Grade | Date |
|---|---|---|---|---|---|---|---|---|---|---|---|
| 01 | | | | | | | | | | | |
| 02 | | | | | | | | | | | |
| 03 | | | | | | | | | | | |
| 04 | | | | | | | | | | | |
| 05 | | | | | | | | | | | |
| 06 | | | | | | | | | | | |
| 07 | | | | | | | | | | | |
| 08 | | | | | | | | | | | |
| 09 | | | | | | | | | | | |
| 10 | | | | | | | | | | | |

# INSTRUCTIONS FOR HISTORY & GEOGRAPHY

The LIFEPAC curriculum from grades two through twelve is structured so that the daily instructional material is written directly into the LIFEPACs. The student is encouraged to read and follow this instructional material in order to develop independent study habits. The teacher should introduce the LIFEPAC to the student, set a required completion schedule, complete teacher checks, be available for questions regarding both content and procedures, administer and grade tests, and develop additional learning activities as desired. Teachers working with several students may schedule their time so that students are assigned to a quiet work activity when it is necessary to spend instructional time with one particular student.

The Teacher Notes section of the Teacher's Guide lists the required or suggested materials for the LIFEPACs and provides additional learning activities for the students. The materials section refers only to LIFEPAC materials and does not include materials which may be needed for the additional activities. Additional learning activities provide a change from the daily school routine, encourage the student's interest in learning and may be used as a reward for good study habits.

# HISTORY & GEOGRAPHY 601

Unit 1: World Geography

# TEACHING NOTES

| MATERIALS NEEDED FOR LIFEPAC | |
|---|---|
| Required | Suggested |
| (None) | • atlas<br>• Bible<br>• dictionary<br>• globe<br>• large maps of North and South America, Europe, the Middle East, Asia, the Soviet Union, Australia, New Zealand, and Antarctica<br>• large map of Southern hemisphere<br>• large map of Western and Eastern hemispheres<br>• reference books or websites |

## ADDITIONAL LEARNING ACTIVITIES

**Section 1: Latitude and Longitude**

1. Discuss these questions with your class.

   a. How can it be Monday in half the world and a different day in the other half of the world?

   b. How many time zones are in the world? (Twenty-four – one for every 15° longitude.)

   c. How many time zones are in the mainland United States? (Four)

2. Use a large wall map of the world or find a world map in an atlas. With one classmate or several, find the longitude and latitude of your home town. Now find the longitude and latitude for these cities:

   | | |
   |---|---|
   | Washington, D.C. | London, England |
   | Phoenix, Arizona | Saigon, Vietnam |
   | Buenos Aires, Argentina | Honolulu, Hawaii |

3. Make at least four clocks out of cardboard. You may place them on one large cardboard if you wish. Put the numbers in the correct places, and make cardboard hands. Fasten the hands to the clocks with brads. Label the clocks Eastern, Central, Mountain, and Pacific. In your time zone set the clock at the hour it is right now. Set the clock in the other United States times zones at their correct hours. Make more clocks and set the hour for Nome, Alaska; Honolulu, Hawaii; Hong Kong; Calcutta, India; Rome, Italy; and Stockholm, Sweden. Be sure to label each clock. You can find time-zone charts in most atlases or online.

4. The Vikings, who were Scandinavian, sailed in the cold seas and landed on the coast of North America. They established three colonies, all of which have disappeared. What could have happened? Famine? War? Desertion? What kind of natives did they deal with? Look up all you can find on the Vikings. Then write and illustrate a story about what you think may have happened.

### Section 2: The Western Hemisphere

1. Discuss these questions with your class.

    a. Why does climate change?

    b. What are glaciers?

    c. What causes the variety of climate? (length of continent)

    d. What is meant by the Continental Divide?

    e. What causes earthquakes? (faults)

    f. What do we mean by the physical features of a continent?

    g. Invite a geologist to speak to the class about earthquakes or invite a meteorologist (professional or hobbyist) to speak to the class about weather patterns. A "ham" radio hobbyist could speak about the distances he contacts with his radio.

2. Get a classmate or classmates to help you find items in newspapers, current news magazines, or reliable online sources about the Panama Canal. Find out if any work is being done on the canal and what is taking place in the government of Panama. Discuss with each other what you have learned.

3. Start a display on the bulletin board of your room or on a large poster to be placed in your room. Entitle it "Our World." On it place pictures you have cut out or drawn of people in North and South America in traditional costumes. Add pictures of special activities, ships, boats, carts, or special foods found on these continents.

### Section 3: The Eastern Hemisphere

1. Discuss this question with your class. Look at the Physical Map of Africa in the LIFEPAC. What divides the continent of Africa in half?

2. Tell the story of Joseph to the children, Genesis chapters 37, 39, 45, and 46:27– chapter 50. Or ask them to read it for themselves. (A good Bible story might be easier for the students.) Discuss why the famine came to this part of the world. In Canaan, natural causes combined with little knowledge of cropraising procedures, and lack of irrigation caused famine. In Egypt famine came, perhaps, because of unwise control of the Nile waters. Be sure to point-out, however, that Egypt had grain. Discuss how this situation could be. Extend discussion to include the manner in which Jacob and his family had to travel to Egypt. In time of famine, was the journey a pleasant one? If famine came in our time, what steps would be taken to alleviate it?

3. With another classmate or classmates make a picture or model of the Suez Canal and the territory surrounding it. Display the model in your classroom.

4. With classmates look up all the news items you can find on the relationships between Egypt and Israel today. Find out from news items the relationship of Israel and Egypt to the countries around them—now called the Arab nations or Arab world. Show your clippings to your teacher and post them on the bulletin board.

5. Find pictures of the people and customs of Africa, Europe, and Asia. Add these pictures to your "Our World" display board.

6. Open the atlas to a world map or research online. Also look at the maps in your LIFEPAC. You may do this activity with another student if you wish. You may have to look at pictures of individual continents. Find these places, rivers, and countries all over our world. See which one can find them first.

| | | |
|---|---|---|
| Red Sea | Philippines | Atlantic Ocean |
| Nile River | Korea | Arctic Ocean |
| Sahara Desert | Vietnam | Shannon River |
| Mt. Kilimanjaro | Japan | Danube River |
| Siberia | Indian Ocean | Dnieper River |
| Manchuria | Australia | Volga River |
| Gobi Desert | Antarctica Ural | Mountains |
| China | Hawaii | Iraq |
| India | Pacific Ocean | Iran |

Did you find all thirty-six names? Many of them appear in later LIFEPACS.

## Section 4: The Southern Hemisphere

1. Locate Tasmania.

2. Discuss these questions with your class.

   a. Has the Antarctic always been a frozen land mass?

   b. Why are the people of Australia and New Zealand, primarily European, mainly British, in background?

   c. What continent has only one national government?

   d. In January of 1978, the first baby was born in Antarctica. You may want to look up the data on this event. Why had no births taken place before? Have there been more? Are there environmental reasons that keep humans from having children there? Who were the lucky parents? Give a written or oral report.

3. If you know of someone in your city from Australia or New Zealand ask him to talk to the students about his native country. Ask someone who has traveled there to tell the students about the countries if you do not know someone who has lived there.

4. With a classmate or classmates look up all you can find about Antarctica. Pool your information. Then make a model or picture diagram of "Little America."

5. Add items about the continents of the Southern Hemisphere to the "Our World" display of customs and people that you already have started.

6. Choose one of the continents you are studying in LIFEPAC 601. Trace the picture of it on the center of a piece of paper. You may trace the maps in your LIFEPAC if you wish. Around the border of your map, paste pictures of the flowers, animals, crops, and natural resources that can be found on that continent. You may do more than one continent if you have the time.

**Section 5: Political and Cultural Regions**

1. Discuss these questions with your class.

    a. What do we mean by a bicameral system of government?

    b. What region of the Americas is called the Anglo-American region?

    c. What do we mean by a political map?

    d. If you were to visit the Middle East today, what contrasts would you see?

    e. What countries are included in the Far East?

    f. What have we received from the ancient Chinese civilization?

    g. What do we mean by the People's Republic of China?

2. With another student interview persons of different racial or national backgrounds than yours. These may be other members of the class, teachers, custodians, neighbors, or friends. When you finish, tell each other what you have found out. Write a short report on some conclusions you have drawn about people who are different from you.

3. With a classmate compose a skit about

    a. being stranded on the desert in summer or

    b. trying to move across the ice floes of the Arctic.

    Be sure to include what you would eat, what you would drink, how you would adjust your clothing to meet the crisis, and other important facts of survival. Do extra reading for this assignment. When you get your skit completed, act it out for the class.

4. Draw a large tree with branches. Label it ROOTS. On a separate piece of scratch paper, write all the relatives on your mother's and on your father's side of the family and where they came from. Ask your parents to help. On the tree trunk copy from your scratch paper the names of the oldest greatgrandparents — on both sides of your cousins.

# ANSWER KEYS

## SECTION 1

| | |
|---|---|
| **1.1** | latitude, parallels |
| **1.2** | equator |
| **1.3** | warmer, higher |
| **1.4** | colder |
| **1.5** | longitude, meridians |
| **1.6** | International Date Line |
| **1.7** | Prime Meridian |
| **1.8** | equator |
| **1.9** | North Pole |
| **1.10** | sphere |

**1.11**  a. Pacific   b. Eastern
       c. Mountain   d. Central

**1.12**  a. Alaska
       b. Hawaii-Aleutian

| | |
|---|---|
| **1.13** | 24 |
| **1.14** | 15° |
| **1.15** | hour and day |
| **1.16** | a |
| **1.17** | f, g |
| **1.18** | d, e |
| **1.19** | b |
| **1.20** | c |
| **1.21** | b |
| **1.22** | g |
| **1.23** | e |
| **1.24** | a |
| **1.25** | d |

## SELF TEST 1

| | |
|---|---|
| **1.01** | Geography |
| **1.02** | equator |
| **1.03** | axis |
| **1.04** | International Date |
| **1.05** | South Pole |
| **1.06** | equator |
| **1.07** | 24 |
| **1.08** | globe |
| **1.09** | Prime Meridian |
| **1.010** | longitude, meridians |
| **1.011** | latitude, parallels |
| **1.012** | International Date Line |
| **1.013** | sphere |
| **1.014** | Northern |
| **1.015** | Southern |
| **1.016** | Eastern |
| **1.017** | Western |
| **1.018** | true |
| **1.019** | false |
| **1.020** | false |
| **1.021** | true |
| **1.022** | false |
| **1.023** | true |
| **1.024** | false |
| **1.025** | false |
| **1.026** | true |
| **1.027** | true |

## SECTION 2

| | |
|---|---|
| **2.1** | Atlantic Ocean |
| **2.2** | north |
| **2.3** | Pacific Ocean |
| **2.4** | Mississippi - Missouri |
| **2.5** | Alaska |
| **2.6** | true |
| **2.7** | true |
| **2.8** | false |
| **2.9** | false |
| **2.10** | true |
| **2.11** | Activities will vary. |
| **2.12** | climate |
| **2.13** | The growing season is short. |
| **2.14** | A long growing season and plentiful rain make better conditions for growing crops. |
| **2.15** | the Westerlies |
| **2.16** | irrigation |
| **2.17** | fourth |
| **2.18** | Caribbean Sea, Atlantic Ocean |
| **2.19** | Amazon |
| **2.20** | Mt. Aconcagua |
| **2.21** | tropical |
| **2.22** | south middle |
| **2.23** | Andes |
| **2.24** | Andes |
| **2.25** | a. mountain |
| | b. south |
| | c. ton |
| | d. east |
| | e. continent |
| | f. west |
| | g. world |
| | h. north |
| | i. region |

## SELF TEST 2

| | |
|---|---|
| **2.01** | north and south |
| **2.02** | equator |
| **2.03** | McKinley |
| **2.04** | Western |
| **2.05** | east |
| **2.06** | four |
| **2.07** | length |
| **2.08** | glacier |
| **2.09** | irrigation |
| **2.010** | over 200 |
| **2.011** | steppes |
| **2.012** | Mississippi - Missouri |
| **2.013** | Amazon |
| **2.014** | Rocky (Rockies) |
| **2.015** | Andes |
| **2.016** | east |
| **2.017** | south |
| **2.018** | earthquakes |
| **2.019** | in the Andes |
| **2.020** | Central America |
| **2.021** | latitude |
| **2.022** | meridians |
| **2.023** | twenty-four |
| **2.024** | 15 |
| **2.025** | International Date Line |
| **2.026** | depress |
| **2.027** | domestic |
| **2.028** | equator |
| **2.029** | progress |
| **2.030** | sediment |
| **2.031** | Imaginary line running north and south which measures the distance east or west of the prime meridian. |
| **2.032** | Imaginary line running east and west which measures the distance north or south of the equator. |
| **2.033** | A large, high plain. |
| **2.034** | A narrow strip of land which connects other lands. |
| **2.035** | The study of the earth's surface, climate, continents, countries, people, industries, and products. |

# SECTION 3

| | |
|---|---|
| **3.1** | Africa is the second largest continent. |
| **3.2** | The Sahara is the great desert of Africa. |
| **3.3** | swiftly |
| **3.4** | The Nile left rich soil. |
| **3.5** | Moses was the baby hidden in the Nile. |
| **3.6** | deserts |
| **3.7** | large |
| **3.8** | tropical |
| **3.9** | mountains |
| **3.10** | The equator runs through the middle |
| **3.11** | Circle a, c, d, f, and g. |
| **3.12** | small |
| **3.13** | middle |
| **3.14** | Alps |
| **3.15** | plain |
| **3.16** | Rhine |
| **3.17** | the Netherlands |
| **3.18** | c |
| **3.19** | a |
| **3.20** | e |
| **3.21** | b |
| **3.22** | d |
| **3.23** | largest |
| **3.24** | civilizations |
| **3.25** | Everest |
| **3.26** | Dead Sea |
| **3.27** | c |
| **3.28** | a |
| **3.29** | d |
| **3.30** | b |

# SELF TEST 3

| | |
|---|---|
| **3.01** | South America |
| **3.02** | Africa |
| **3.03** | Europe |
| **3.04** | North America |
| **3.05** | Asia |
| **3.06** | South America |
| **3.07** | Asia |
| **3.08** | North America |
| **3.09** | Europe |
| **3.010** | Africa |
| **3.011** | false |
| **3.012** | false |
| **3.013** | true |
| **3.014** | true |
| **3.015** | false |
| **3.016** | false |
| **3.017** | true |
| **3.018** | true |
| **3.019** | true |
| **3.020** | false |
| **3.021** | true |
| **3.022** | false |
| **3.023** | true |
| **3.024** | true |
| **3.025** | true |
| **3.026** | ✓ |
| **3.027** | ✓ |
| **3.028** | |
| **3.029** | ✓ |
| **3.030** | ✓ |
| **3.031** | |
| **3.032** | |
| **3.033** | ✓ |
| **3.034** | |
| **3.035** | |
| **3.036** | The swiftly flowing water from the highlands prevents the rivers from having good harbors, although Capetown and Cairo are exceptions. |
| **3.037** | Temperate climate, middle latitudes ample rainfall, and fertile soil would make the best farmland. |
| **3.038** | If both the longitude and latitude of a certain place are known, you can locate the place where the two lines cross. |
| **3.039** | Geography is the study of the earth's surface, climate, continents, countries, people, industries, and products. |

# SECTION 4

| | |
|---|---|
| **4.1** | Southern |
| **4.2** | east |
| **4.3** | the Tropic of Capricorn |
| **4.4** | Great Dividing Range |
| **4.5** | true |
| **4.6** | false |
| **4.7** | true |
| **4.8** | false |
| **4.9** | It is too cold for snow to melt and form rivers. |
| **4.10** | The climate is colder because of the high elevation and the strong winds. |
| **4.11** | g |
| **4.12** | h |
| **4.13** | e |
| **4.14** | j |
| **4.15** | i |
| **4.16** | f |
| **4.17** | b |
| **4.18** | c |
| **4.19** | d |
| **4.20** | a |

# SELF TEST 4

| | |
|---|---|
| **4.01** | Antarctica |
| **4.02** | Australia |
| **4.03** | Asia |
| **4.04** | Africa |
| **4.05** | North America |
| **4.06** | Africa |
| **4.07** | North America |
| **4.08** | Europe |
| **4.09** | South America |
| **4.010** | Antarctica |
| **4.011** | Either order: <br> North America <br> South America |
| **4.012** | Any order: <br> Asia <br> Africa <br> Europe <br> Australia |
| **4.013** | Either order: <br> Australia <br> Antarctica |
| **4.014** | Asia |
| **4.015** | Mt. Everest |
| **4.016** | Asia |
| **4.017** | dry |
| **4.018** | winds |
| **4.019** | tropical |
| **4.020** | ice |
| **4.021** | lines of longitude or meridians |
| **4.022** | the equator |
| **4.023** | It is the same spherical shape as the earth. |
| **4.024** | Fossils have been found. |
| **4.025** | The rain falls on the coastal mountain ranges. |

# SECTION 5 :

| | |
|---|---|
| **5.1** | English |
| **5.2** | friendly |
| **5.3** | skill |
| **5.4** | high |
| **5.5** | Spanish and Portuguese |
| **5.6** | older |
| **5.7** | rain forests |
| **5.8** | products |
| **5.9** | false |
| **5.10** | false |
| **5.11** | true |
| **5.12** | He has given them many minerals. |
| **5.13** | The tribes fight each other. |
| **5.14** | Africans would share a common Master in Jesus. They would be more willing to practice Christian principles. |
| **5.15** | d |
| **5.16** | e |
| **5.17** | c |
| **5.18** | b |
| **5.19** | a |
| **5.20** | European countries ruled so many other countries of the world. |
| **5.21** | Latin America |
| **5.22** | A group of countries in western Europe which are joining together to form a united Europe. |
| **5.23** | Either order: old, new |
| **5.24** | oil |
| **5.25** | Holy Land, birthplace of Christianity |
| **5.26** | Christianity |
| **5.27** | Middle East |
| **5.28** | animals, crops |
| **5.29** | false |
| **5.30** | true |
| **5.31** | true |
| **5.32** | false |
| **5.33** | true |
| **5.34** | largest |
| **5.35** | harsh |
| **5.36** | communist |
| **5.37** | dissidents |
| **5.38** | rewards |
| **5.39** | Australia |
| **5.40** | a trade |
| **5.41** | the British |
| **5.42** | Either order:<br>a. social security<br>b. give women the right to vote |
| **5.43** | the Maoris |

# SELF TEST 5

| | |
|---|---|
| **5.01** | true |
| **5.02** | true |
| **5.03** | false |
| **5.04** | false |
| **5.05** | true |
| **5.06** | true |
| **5.07** | false |
| **5.08** | true |
| **5.09** | true |
| **5.010** | true |
| **5.011** | true |
| **5.012** | false |
| **5.013** | false |
| **5.014** | true |
| **5.015** | false |
| **5.016** | false |
| **5.017** | false |
| **5.018** | true |
| **5.019** | false |
| **5.020** | true |
| **5.021** | i |
| **5.022** | d |
| **5.023** | a |
| **5.024** | b |
| **5.025** | j |
| **5.026** | h |
| **5.027** | c |
| **5.028** | e |
| **5.029** | f |
| **5.030** | g |
| **5.031** | longitude |
| **5.032** | Prime Meridian |
| **5.033** | Pacific |
| **5.034** | glacier |
| **5.035** | South |
| **5.036** | second |
| **5.037** | Asia |
| **5.038** | communist |
| **5.039** | c |
| **5.040** | Countries in Europe ruled over many of the countries of the world at one time. Many people of Europe have moved to other countries. |
| **5.041** | The interior of Australia is hot and dry because the rain falls on the coastal mountain ranges. |

# LIFEPAC TEST

| | |
|---|---|
| 1. | k |
| 2. | f |
| 3. | h |
| 4. | b |
| 5. | j |
| 6. | k |
| 7. | i |
| 8. | f |
| 9. | k |
| 10. | a |
| 11. | true |
| 12. | false |
| 13. | false |
| 14. | true |
| 15. | true |
| 16. | true |
| 17. | true |
| 18. | true |
| 19. | true |
| 20. | false |
| 21. | false |
| 22. | c. twenty-four |
| 23. | a. equator |
| 24. | a. Greenwich, England |

| | | |
|---|---|---|
| 25. | c. | Russia |
| 26. | c. | better living conditions |
| 27. | a. | 8 |
| | b. | 7 |
| | c. | 6 |
| | d. | 2 |
| | e. | 4 |
| | f. | 3 |
| | g. | 1 |
| 28. | c. | Communist nation |
| 29. | c. | technical skills |
| 30. | b. | Canada |
| 31. | b. | Panama Canal |
| 32. | | rotates |
| 33. | | parallels |
| 34. | | Social Security |
| 35. | | Anglo-America |
| 36. | | meridians |
| 37. | | They have the same type of government. They belong to the British Commonwealth. |
| 38. | a. | Antarctica |
| | b. | Europe |
| | c. | South America |

# ALTERNATE LIFEPAC TEST

1.  a
2.  f
3.  e
4.  g
5.  f
6.  d
7.  g
8.  c
9.  e
10. b
11. true
12. true
13. true
14. true
15. true
16. false
17. true
18. false
19. false
20. false
21. b.  four
22. c.  a day
23. c.  equator

24. a.  Scandinavia
25. b.  Anglo-America
26. a.  Latin America
27. b.  Greenland
28. a.  Mississippi-Missouri river system
29. b.  their tribes
30. a.  Asia
31. rice
32. Panama
33. school
34. East
35. Africa
36. Europe
37. North Pole
38. globe
39. English
40. Japan
41. Full sentences should include imaginary lines; equator at 0°; run east and west; parallels
40. Full sentences should include meridians; run north and south; imaginary; Prime Meridian at 0°; used for time zones

# HISTORY & GEOGRAPHY 601

## ALTERNATE LIFEPAC TEST

**NAME** _____

**DATE** _____

**SCORE** _____

**Match these items, answers may be used more than once** (each answer, 2 points).

1. _____ is in the Northern and Western hemispheres

2. _____ in the Eastern and Southern henispheres

3. _____ has the great Sahara Desert and lies in the Eastern Hemisphere

4. _____ surrounds the South Pole

5. _____ the smallest continent with close ties to Britain

6. _____ contains India

7. _____ once a tropical land

8. _____ contains Ireland, Spain, and Italy

9. _____ most countries became independent after 1950

10. _____ equator crosses it in Western Hemisphere

a. North America

b. South America

c. Europe

d. Asia

e. Africa

f. Australia

g. Antarctica

h. Western Hemisphere

i. Eastern Hemisphere

**Answer true or false** (each answer, 2 points).

11. _____ North America is in the Western Hemisphere.

12. _____ Africa is in the Eastern Hemisphere.

13. _____ Asia is in the Eastern Hemisphere.

14. _____ The longest river in North America is the Mississippi River.

15. _____ The largest river in South America is the Amazon.

16. _____ The Nile River is in South America.

17. _____ The Rhine River is Europe's most important river.

18. _____ The Sahara Desert is in South America.

19. _____ There are five continents in the world.

20. _____ Twenty time zones have been established around the world.

**Write the correct letter and answer on each blank** (each answer, 2 points).

21. The United States mainland has _____ time zones.
    a. three            b. four            c. five

22. One may lose or gain _____ when flying across the International Dateline.
    a. seventy minutes    b. two hours        c. a day

23. The low, or hot latitudes, are close to the _____ .
    a. 50° S. latitude      b. Arctic Circle      c. equator

24. The region of Europe with a social security system is _____ .
    a. Scandinavia        b. Middle East        c. the Orient

25. Canada, the United States, and Greenland are called _____ .
    a. Latin America      b. Anglo-America      c. Colonial America

26. The Spanish-Portuguese language and customs unite _____ .
    a. Latin America      b. Europe            c. Africa

27. The Island of the Anglo-American region is _____ .
    a. Iceland            b. Greenland          c. Hawaiian Islands

28. The greatest river system in North America is the _____ .
    a. Mississippi-Missouri river system
    b. Yukon River
    c. Panama Canal

29. In Africa the people are most loyal to _____ .
    a. Britain            b. their tribes        c. their country

30. The largest continent is _____ .
    a. Asia                       b. Europe                       c. Africa

**Complete these statements** (each answer, 3 points).

31. The "staff of life" for most of the Far East is _____ .

32. The Panama Canal cuts through the Isthmus of _____ .

33. Australia's education is free, and all children must go to _____ .

34. Jerusalem is part of the Middle _____ .

35. Egypt is part of the continent of _____ .

36. Great Britain is part of the continent of _____ .

37. The _____ is located at 90° north latitude.

38. The best map of the earth is a _____ .

39. The chief language of the Anglo-American countries is _____ .

40. The Far East country that was defeated in World War II and has become an industrial giant is _____ .

**Answer these questions** (each answer, 5 points).

41. Give a complete explanation of the word *latitude*, giving another name for it.

    _____

    _____

    _____

41. Explain the word *longitude*, give another name for it, and name an important function these lines perform for the world.

    _____

    _____

    _____

    _____

# HISTORY & GEOGRAPHY 602

Unit 2: The Cradle of Civilization

# TEACHING NOTES

| MATERIALS NEEDED FOR LIFEPAC | |
| --- | --- |
| Required | Suggested |
| (None) | • Bible<br>• dictionary<br>• globe<br>• large map including Fertile Crescent<br>• large map of Israel<br>• reference books or websites |

## ADDITIONAL LEARNING ACTIVITIES

**Section 1: Mesopotamia**

1. Encourage each student to develop an honest appraisal of his own work.

2. Seek to develop in the student an appreciation of the contributions made by past civilizations.

3. Discuss with your class these questions.

   a. How does the study of this LIFEPAC help you understand the Bible?

   b. What people and places in this LIFEPAC have you heard mentioned in the Bible?

   c. How did the rich soil in the fertile Crescent affect the development of civilization?

   d. Why was the Fertile Crescent the cause of wars?

   e. What do we mean by *civilization*?

   f. Look at the map of The Fertile Crescent. Compare it with a modern map of this area. How have the countries and locations changed today?

4. Write a short article as if you had helped to build the Hanging Gardens of Babylon. Tell the names of the friends who worked with you. What kind of work did you do? Were you paid? How? How was the water taken to the top terraces? Illustrate. (This project can be done by students in groups or as a class.)

5. With classmates pretend you lived in Babylon when the Assyrians invaded and what happened. Where were you and how did you live through the struggle? Discuss among yourselves.

6. Look up information on Nineveh. Read the Bible story of Jonah. Write a skit including information about Nineveh. Give the skit to the class, or you and

7. Write a story about a student in one of the early cities of Mesopotamia. Tell about his home life, his meals, his school, and his religion. Use pictures for words and write from right to left.

8. Draw a picture of events that took place in the ziggurat temples.

9. Draw an Assyrian chariot or draw some iron weapons.

10. Design a Persian textile. Study Persian styles of designs first.

**Section 2: Israel**

1.  Discuss with the students these questions.

    a.  How have God's people (the Jews) been mistreated through the years?

    b.  What is a big problem in Israel? (water) What are modern Israelis doing about this problem?

    c.  Of what value is the Dead Sea?

    d.  Who are Zionists?

2.  Have the class read Deuteronomy 5:7–21. Teacher should discuss with students the meaning of each commandment. Write on the blackboard the core meaning of each commandment.

3.  The Ten Commandments could be read together for a choral reading. For instance, divide group into high and low voices (girls and boys). Alternate the voices, with a solo now and then. Music could be used as a background. For a backdrop a large slab of stone against a desert scene could be painted.

4.  Read the story of David and Goliath in the Bible (1 Samuel 17:20–58). Write a play. The following outline is suggested:

    Scene 1—David asks Saul's permission to destroy Goliath (1 Samuel 17:20–40). Let David tell his reasons for wanting to go. Then show the preparation.

    Scene 2—The battle (1 Samuel 17:41–53). Show and tell what David said and did.

    Scene-3—The return to Saul (1 Samuel 17:54–58). David takes Goliath's head to Saul. What does Saul say? What does David tell? Practice the skit and present it to the class.

5.  Look for more information about the Dead Sea. Is the Great Salt Lake in Utah similar? Tell a classmate what you have learned about the Dead Sea or write a report.

6.  Make a booklet of the Ten Commandments. Either draw or cut out pictures for illustrations.

7.  Look in your daily newspaper or online to find current reports about the conditions in Israel. Make a scrapbook or mount the clippings or printouts on the bulletin board in your room.

**Section 3: Egypt**

1.  Discuss these questions with your class.

    a.  Why is the land along the Nile so rich?

    b.  What made Egypt so attractive to early man?

    c.  Why is the Great Pyramid considered to be one of the Seven Wonders of the World?

    d.  What has happened to many of the temple ruins along the Nile?

    e.  What kind of ruler was Queen Hatshepsut?

    f.  In Hebrews 11:24–26 you read about Moses. What riches did Moses forsake to obey God?

    g.  How did advisors help the pharaohs?

    h.  In Egypt how were seasons judged?

    i.  What is polytheism?

    j.  What is monotheism?

    k.  Why did powerful rulers resent the preaching of one true God?

2. Using papier-mâché, make a mummy to resemble King Tut or another pharaoh. To make papier-mâché, tear newspapers into pieces, mix with glue and water until you have a soft consistency. Use balloons, tied together, or shaped chicken wire or even a plank of wood for a base. Read about how mummies were preserved and try to get yours to resemble the real thing. After the papier-mâché has dried, paint your mummy. Put a mask on it as they did in ancient Egypt.

3. Look at a map of the modern Fertile Crescent. With a classmate, study it carefully. Discuss these questions with each other.

    a. What countries now border the Tigris and Euphrates rivers?

    b. Compare the map of The Fertile Crescent in Section 1 with a modern map of the regions shown. Where are the boundaries of Egypt now in comparison to early days?

    c. In what way is Israel different?

    d. Did Russia exist in Bible times?

    e. What other observations can you make?

    You may have had a class discussion on this subject. If so, review what you have learned.

4. Look up in books, magazines, or online the kind of jewelry used by both men and women in ancient Egypt. Out of plastic lids, or other plastic, fashion an ornament similar to those you find. You may wish to glue on old beads or sequins for decoration. What kind of insect did Egyptians use for good-luck jewelry? See if you can make one out of papier-mâché or clay. Paint it.

5. Draw a large picture of one of the treasures of King Tut's tomb. Some pictures can be found in magazines, books, and encyclopedias. After drawing them color them. Display your picture on the wall of your room at school.

# STUDENT WORKSHEET

The following activity may be reproduced as a student worksheet.

## » ANSWER KEY

| | |
|---|---|
| Exodus 7:10 | flood |
| Exodus 7:20 | waters turned to blood |
| Exodus 8:6 | plague of frogs |
| Exodus 8:17 | plague of lice |
| Exodus 8:24 | plague of flies |
| Exodus 9:6 | Egypt's cattle died, but not Israel's |
| Exodus 9:10 | plague of boils |
| Exodus 9:23, 24 | rain of hail and fire |
| Exodus 9:13-15 | Lord promises plagues on Egypt |
| Exodus 10:22-23 | plague of darkness |
| Exodus 12:29 | death of all the first born |
| Exodus 14:21-28 | parting of the Red Sea waters |

## » THE MIRACLES OF MOSES

When Moses was called of God to free the Israelites from Egypt, many strange plagues and miracles came to the land of Egypt because the Pharaoh's heart was so hard. Look up the following Bible verses and put down beside each of them which plague or miracle is mentioned in this reference.

| Reference | Plague or Miracle |
|---|---|
| Exodus 7:10 | _____ |
| Exodus 7:20 | _____ |
| Exodus 8:6 | _____ |
| Exodus 8:17 | _____ |
| Exodus 8:24 | _____ |
| Exodus 9:6 | _____ |
| Exodus 9:10 | _____ |
| Exodus 9:23 and 24 | _____ |
| Exodus 9:13–15 | _____ |
| Exodus 10:22 and 23 | _____ |
| Exodus 12:29 | _____ |
| Exodus 14:8 | _____ |

**Answer these questions on a separate sheet of paper.**

Do you think any of these miracles were the result of natural causes that might have happened anyway? Which one of the plagues made the Pharaoh finally give in and let the Israelites go? Why was it necessary for the Red Sea to be parted if the Pharaoh told them they could leave? Why did they not leave in an orderly, leisurely fashion? Why do you suppose the Pharaoh wanted to keep the Israelites in Egypt? Do you think the fact that most Israelites were good, hard, intelligent workers have anything to do with it?

When you finish, show it to your teacher; then put it in your folder.

# ANSWER KEYS

## SECTION 1

**1.1** The Fertile Crescent is in southwestern Asia.
**1.2** The Biblical name is Paddan-Aram
**1.3** Many other tribes wanted the rich soil.
**1.4** Sumer
**1.5** Akkad
**1.6** Sargon I
**1.7** Abraham
**1.8** Ur became part of the desert.
**1.9** The land was very flat.
**1.10** write, to trade, to use metal and to live in villages.
**1.11** priests and kings
**1.12** geometry
**1.13** cylinders
**1.14** Inanna
**1.15** date
**1.16** libraries
**1.17** coins
**1.18** eternal
**1.19** The young must be well trained to carry on the knowledge and skills, or all is forgotten.
**1.20** Babylonia
**1.21** Code of Hammurabi
**1.22** The stone is in the Louvre, Paris, France.
**1.23** Marriages were made legal by written contracts.
**1.24** Cuneiform was the kind of writing used by the Babylonians.
**1.25** split-level
**1.26** Ziggurats
**1.27** astronomy
**1.28** Lebanon
**1.29** many gods
**1.30** They had better equipment including the horse and chariot and iron weapons.
**1.31** Most women would choose to live in Sumer because of the cruel treatment of woman in Assyria.
**1.32** horse
**1.33** There would be fewer people to rebel.
**1.34** They traded with other countries that had iron.
**1.35** true
**1.36** true
**1.37** true
**1.38** false
**1.39** false
**1.40** He permitted them to go home.
**1.41** People could travel and learn from each other.
**1.42** The Persians had metal.
**1.43** The Divine right of kings was a belief that kingly authority comes from God.
**1.44** yes, very
**1.45** A country must maintain justice, good education, and morals to remain great.
**1.46** a. against slavery
b. a belief in many gods
c. having one rail
d. having one tone
e. not stable
f. not dependent on others
g. to make new again
h. to go toward
i. to write again
j. a test given before
k. pertaining to agriculture
l. toward the east
m. a system of symbols
n. one who studies archeology
o. without joy
p. having to do with a disaster
q. without a god

# SELF TEST 1

**1.01**  fertile land
open, flat land
rich soil
between the Tigris and Euphrates River
sufficient water
**1.02**  b
**1.03**  a
**1.04**  a
**1.05**  b
**1.06**  b
**1.07**  b
**1.08**  a
**1.09**  a.  Persia
     b.  Assyria
     c.  Chaldea
     d.  Babylonia
     e.  Sumer
**1.010**  They were interested in the rich farmland of the Fertile Crescent.
**1.011**  civilized
**1.012**  Ur
**1.013**  mud bricks or bundles of reeds
**1.014**  writing
**1.015**  written code of laws
**1.016**  ziggurats
**1.017**  split-level
**1.018**  the Hanging Gardens of Babylon
**1.019**  many gods
**1.020**  Persians

# SECTION 2

**2.1**  Palestine and Canaan are two other names for Israel.
**2.2**  The land is not suitable for farming.
**2.3**  The Dead Sea is the lowest place on any continent.
**2.4**  Jesus often preached around the Sea of Galilee.
**2.5**  The Jordan River runs north and south in Israel.
**2.6**  Jacob left Canaan because of famine and drought.
**2.7**  They were made slaves.
**2.8**  Moses led the Hebrews out of Egypt.
**2.9**  They were rulers of Israel.
**2.10**  Israel in the north and Judah in the south existed during the Split Kingdom.
**2.11**  Jerusalem was destroyed several times.
**2.12**  They had no country.
**2.13**  He was an Austrian writer who started the Zionist Organization.
**2.14**  The terrible event was the killing of 6,000,000 Jews.
**2.15**  Any order:
     a.  The Jews were the first people to believe in one God.
     b.  The Jews have made contributions in Hebrew literature.
     c.  The Jews have been an example of courage.
     d.  They have established work programs in the Kibbutz.
     e.  The Jews have developed the country of Israel.
**2.16**  Haifa and Tel-Aviv are two important cities.
**2.17**  2.  longingly
     2.  severely
     2.  skimpily
     2.  sufficiently
     2.  ruthlessly
     2.  skillfully
     2.  quietly
     2.  cruelly

# SELF TEST 2

**2.01** true
**2.02** false
**2.03** true
**2.04** true
**2.05** false
**2.06** true
**2.07** false
**2.08** false
**2.09** true
**2.010** true
**2.011** a. religion
**2.012** b. law-making body
**2.013** b. Egypt
**2.014** c. Moses
**2.015** b. most industrial
**2.016** geography
**2.017** contribution or history
**2.018** contribution
**2.019** geography
**2.020** history
**2.021** history
**2.022** geography
**2.023** history
**2.024** geography
**2.025** geography
**2.026** a. Palestine
b. Canaan or Zion
**2.027** geometry
**2.028** Code of Hammurabi
**2.029** cuneiform
**2.030** Example:
The children must be well trained to carry on the knowledge and skills, or all is forgotten.
**2.031** Israel existed in the north and Judah existed in the south during the split kingdom.
**2.032** The Fertile Crescent is in southwestern Asia.

# SECTION 3

**3.1** The delta had rich soil, a warm climate, and plenty of water.
**3.2** The land which is rich farm land is deposited by the Nile.
**3.3** The Great Pyramid was built.
**3.4** Ka was the soul of man.
**3.5** It is the huge stone creature with a man's head and a lion's body
**3.6** Amenemhet I reunited Egypt.
**3.7** The Hyksos brought the horse and chariot to Egypt.
**3.8** He was the god of afterlife and vegetation.
**3.9** The Egyptians secured gold and silver from Nubia.
**3.10** Amosis I overthrew the Hyksos.
**3.11** Aton
**3.12** valley of the Kings
**3.13** his aunt's work
**3.14** benevolent
**3.15** Tutankhamen
**3.16** The dead needed them in the afterlife.
**3.17** many
**3.18** torture
**3.19** letters
**3.20** credit
**3.21** b. saws
c. razors
d. tools
g. furniture
h. bottles
**3.22** thirty
**3.23** beetle
**3.24** superior
**3.25** Stories will vary.

## SELF TEST 3

| | |
|---|---|
| **3.01** | l |
| **3.02** | k |
| **3.03** | i |
| **3.04** | f |
| **3.05** | o |
| **3.06** | e |
| **3.07** | j |
| **3.08** | g |
| **3.09** | c |
| **3.010** | a |
| **3.011** | h |
| **3.012** | d |
| **3.013** | n |
| **3.014** | p |
| **3.015** | false |
| **3.016** | true |
| **3.017** | false |
| **3.018** | true |
| **3.019** | true |
| **3.020** | split-level |
| **3.021** | Egypt |
| **3.022** | the Hanging gardens of Babylon |
| **3.023** | Ur |
| **3.024** | Jews |
| **3.025** | Moses |
| **3.026** | Great Sphinx |
| **3.027** | writing |

**3.028** Any order:
  a. The Jews were the first people to believe in one God.
  b. The Jews have made contributions in Hebrew literature.
  c. The Jews have been an example of courage.
  d. They have established work programs in the kibbutz.
  e. The Jews have developed the country of Israel.

**3.029** He permitted them to go home.

**3.030** Israel existed in the north and Judah existed in the south during the split kingdom.

## LIFEPAC TEST

| | |
|---|---|
| **1.** | rich soil |
| **2.** | settled |
| **3.** | Hebrews |
| **4.** | write |
| **5.** | cuneiform |
| **6.** | Hammurabi |
| **7.** | polytheism |
| **8.** | ziggurats |
| **9.** | f |
| **10.** | e |
| **11.** | a |
| **12.** | c |
| **13.** | d |
| **14.** | g |
| **15.** | i |
| **16.** | h |
| **17.** | b |
| **18.** | j |
| **19.** | m |
| **20.** | k |
| **21.** | psalms |
| **22.** | tombs |
| **23.** | Ra |
| **24.** | Hebrews |
| **25.** | 12 months of 30 days each. |
| **26.** | Dead Sea |
| **27.** | young pharaoh of Egypt |
| **28.** | god of Egypt |
| **29.** | woman pharaoh |
| **30.** | Moses lead the Hebrews home |
| **31.** | lion's body |
| **32.** | Egypt |
| **33.** | Hebrews |
| **34.** | Examples:<br>the Ten Commandments<br>one God<br>the Old Testament |

# ALTERNATE LIFEPAC TEST

| | | | | |
|---|---|---|---|---|
| **1.** | true | **21.** | d | |
| **2.** | false | **22.** | e | |
| **3.** | true | **23.** | f | |
| **4.** | true | **24.** | a | |
| **5.** | true | **25.** | c | |
| **6.** | true | **26.** | b | |
| **7.** | true | **27.** | i | |
| **8.** | true | **28.** | j | |
| **9.** | false | **29.** | h | |
| **10.** | false | **30.** | g | |
| **11.** | Greece | **31.** | b. | Egyptians |
| **12.** | Hammurabi | **32.** | c. | Assyrians |
| **13.** | stone | **33.** | a. | believed in an afterlife |
| **14.** | Ur | **34.** | b. | plagues |
| **15.** | Hanging Gardens of Babylon | **35.** | c. | people want basic rights |
| **16.** | ziggurat | **36.** | b. | two or three stories |
| **17.** | Pyramid | **37.** | b. | law-making body |
| **18.** | salt | **38.** | c. | war-loving people |
| **19.** | diseases | **39.** | b. | the most industrial city of Israel |
| **20.** | Negeb | **40.** | b. | the Great Sphinx was placed nearby |

# HISTORY & GEOGRAPHY 602

## ALTERNATE LIFEPAC TEST

**NAME** _____

**DATE** _____

**SCORE** _____

**Write true or false** (each answer, 2 points).

1. _____ The Fertile Crescent includes land along the Nile River.

2. _____ Mesopotamia had few conquerors.

3. _____ The first writers wrote from right to left.

4. _____ The early people needed a warm climate as well as water and fertile soil.

5. _____ Israel is the modern name for Palestine.

6. _____ Jacob's family was the first Hebrew family in Egypt.

7. _____ *Cuneiform writing* means *wedge-shaped writing*.

8. _____ The Holy City is Jerusalem.

9. _____ The Dead Sea is on high land.

10. _____ The Tigris and Euphrates rivers are in Israel.

**Write the correct word on the line** (each answer, 4 points).

11. The name *Mesopotamia* came from the country of _____ .

12. The name of the king of Babylon who wrote a code of laws was _____ .

13. The laws of Babylon were written on an eight-foot piece of _____ .

14. Abraham, the founder of the Hebrew nation, once lived in the Chaldean city of

_____ .

15. The beautiful gift that Nebuchadnezzar II built for his homesick wife was the _____ .

**16.** A terraced pyramid in Chaldea, used for worship and a market place, is _____ .

**17.** A huge triangular building, used as a tomb for a great pharaoh of Egypt, is called the Great

_____ .

**18.** From the Dead Sea is mined a great quantity of _____ .

**19.** Ancient Egyptian doctors had cures for many _____ .

**20.** One of the world's hottest places, a desert in Israel, is named the _____ .

**Match these items** (each answer, 2 points).

**21.** _____ Assyrians

**22.** _____ Chaldeans

**23.** _____ Sumerians

**24.** _____ Sea of Galilee

**25.** _____ ka

**26.** _____ Ramses II

**27.** _____ loincloths

**28.** _____ Hebrews

**29.** _____ Hatshepsut

**30.** _____ Torah

a. is in the area of Israel with the most moisture

b. made slaves of the Hebrews

c. the name for soul in Egypt

d. tortured their captives in cruel ways

e. invented the iron point on a plow

f. wrote from right to left

g. Jewish Bible (first five books)

h. Egypt's queen with a false beard

i. Egyptian dress

j. without a homeland for two thousand years

k. pillars

**Write the correct letter and answer on the line** (each answer, 2 points).

**31.** Women had the most rights under the laws of the _____ .
   a. Babylonians          b. Egyptians          c. Sumerians

**32.** Women had the fewest rights under the laws of the _____ .
   a. Sumerians          b. Chaldeans          c. Assyrians

**33.** Pharaohs wanted possessions buried with them because they _____ .
   a. believed in an afterlife
   b. wanted to keep them safe
   c. wanted no one else to own them

**34.** When Ramses II refused to let the Hebrews go, God sent many _____ .
   a. storms          b. plagues          c. floods

**35.** The reason slaves are not used in most modern countries is that

_____ .

    a.  machinery does all the work

    b.  there are no illiterates

    c.  people want basic rights

**36.** The temples in which the Babylonians worshiped were _____ .

    a.  flat structures              b.  two or three stories         c.  split-level

**37.** The Knesset is modern Israels's _____ .

    a.  most popular leader        b.  law-making body         c.  northern section

**38.** The Assyrians were a _____ .

    a.  peace-loving people        b.  weak people          c.  war-loving people

**39.** Tel-Aviv of today can be described as _____ .

    a.  the most Christian city of Israel

    b.  the most industrial city of Israel

    c.  the best seaport city in Israel

**40.** To guard the pyramids, _____ .

    a.  soldiers stood outside

    b.  the Great Sphinx was placed nearby

    c.  the figure of a lion was formed

# HISTORY & GEOGRAPHY 603

Unit 3: The Civilizations of Greece and Rome

# TEACHING NOTES

| MATERIALS NEEDED FOR LIFEPAC | |
| --- | --- |
| Required | Suggested |
| (None) | • Bible<br>• map of Greece and Rome or the ancient world<br>• thesaurus<br>• (the reference materials can be either in book or online formats) |

## ADDITIONAL LEARNING ACTIVITIES

**Section 1: The Civilization of Greece**

1. Discuss these questions with your class.

   a. Do you feel geography influences our lives here in (your city or state)?

   b. Do you understand how the shallow soil and steep mountains influenced Greek culture? Try to explain.

   c. Do you think airplane travel and heavy duty farm equipment (had it been available then) would have made things different for the Greek cultures?

   d. Do you think the island of Crete had any influence on the culture?

   e. How much influence might the Spartans have had on the Greek culture?

   f. Do you think the philosophers (Socrates, Plato, and Aristotle) influenced Greek culture?

   g. Do you recognize any Greek architecture here in our town?

   h. Do you see a direct relationship between America's system of democracy and experiments in democracy in Greece?

   i. Do you think the Greeks were the first to discover geography?

2. Visit the library or search online and gather a series of pictures of the Greek peninsula. Photocopy or print out the pictures and then compose a poster for the school with captions beneath each picture. Color the pictures for a more attractive display.

3. You and your classmates pretend your classroom, or other area, is the Greek peninsula. Divide yourselves into four groups (or only two if necessary). Imagine each group is a city-state of ancient Greece. Each group huddle to decide what your needs or desires are as a city-state of Greece. When time is called (five minutes), the leader of each group will stand up and say the needs his group had decided upon. All leaders talk at once, trying to outdo each other! Can anyone make his voice heard? Sit down together quietly. Discuss the fact that the ancient city-states all clamored for themselves much the same way. Do you now have insight into the reason Greece took so long to unite as a nation? How much does the fact that mountains and coastlines divided much of Greece have to do with it?

4. Visit your local courthouse. How many traces of the Greek past can you discover there? You will have to look at the buildings, ask questions of judges and clerks, and so forth. Read again the section on Contributions in your LIFEPAC so that you will have questions ready for

this trip. You may besurprised at how well our democratic process works. Write a report of your trip when it is over.

5. Make a three-dimensional map of Greece with papier-mâché, salt clay, or other material.

6. Work up a "Tale of Three Valleys in Greece." You must look at a good map. Describe the life of a twelve-year-old in each of these valleys. Show how each child's life style might have been different--research this part. Now, conduct an imaginary news broadcast or radio program. Let your fellow classmates know by this means what you have learned.

7. Try writing a letter as the Apostle Paul would have written it to Thomas or another Apostle who took the message of Christ to the Far East. Will there be a difference in the way the message was received from Paul in Greece and the way it was accepted in India? Your minister might be able to help you with this project.

8. Start a poster entitled "CONTRIBUTIONS." To the left of the poster list the contributions of Greece to our world mentioned in the LIFEPAC. Add any others you know about. Illustrate with pictures or drawings if you wish.

## Section 2: The Civilizations of Rome

1. Discuss these questions with your class.

   a. Italy and Greece were mountainous. How did the mountains of Italy differ from those of Greece?

   b. Would the geography of northern Italy and that of southern Italy have made a difference in the life styles of the people of these areas?

   c. From the start the Romans seemed quite civilized. How much of an influence do you suppose the Etruscans were on the Romans? Do you think their life style and way of solving problems were used by the Romans?

   d. All but one of the Apostles were finally martyred. Did Roman law protect the Apostles from quicker deaths than they eventually suffered?

   e. Augustus was a great and wise emperor. He ruled the Roman Empire for forty-four years. Why did Roman civilization begin to decline after his death?

   f. Do you think scientific agricultural techniques or a strong law enforcement (police force) could have prevented Rome's collapse?

2. On the playground construct a three-dimensional map of Italy (use chairs for mountains; mountains should be the primary concern). Let a group represent (a) Romans, (b) northern savages, (c) Sicilians (let each group locate himself properly on the "map"). Analyze the advantages and disadvantages each group had in terms of successfully making war and of defending its land.

3. Stage a public debate, putting the Gracchi brothers against the Patricians. Let the Gracchis argue the point *We have to live (as a nation) for tomorrow*; let the Patricians take the position *It is enough to live for today*. (Read *The century of confusion* again for the context.)

4. A team of students may draw a mural depicting the decay of the Roman civilization.

5. Create a relief map of Italy, portraying in particular the mountains. (Be careful to accent the height of the Alps.)

6. Select a book from the library at the reading level you like best. The book must be on life in the Roman Empire. Write a book report on paper or make an oral report.

7. Become a radio announcer. After finding all the information you can about brick roads, aqueducts, and bridges, report life in America today as if the stone or brick roads or aqueducts or bridges had never been invented or built by the Romans. Keep our civilization as it is, except omit roads, water conduits, or bridges across rivers. Practice this project for your teacher or your parents at home. They could probably help you with suggestions.

8. Fill out the right side, Rome, of the poster you started on "CONTRIBUTIONS." The LIFEPAC in Section 2 mentions many contributions of the Romans to present-day life. Display poster in your room.

## ADDITIONAL INFORMATION

No writing assignment is printed in LIFEPAC 603. Therefore, the teacher should assign an extended writing assignment to the student. Here are suggestions for topics:

    a. The Golden Age of Greece, Athens or Sparta

    b. The contributions of the Greeks

Be sure the student gives a title (properly spelled) to his report and that he leaves neat margins on each side of the paper. Has he capitalized letters properly, and is his handwriting legible? Of course the piece should not be copied but well written in the student's own words. Does the report, or essay, make a point?

If the student wishes to pick a topic of his own from LIFEPAC 603, be sure he checks with the teacher before starting research. Teacher must check the work when student finishes.

## STUDENT WORKSHEETS

Two activity sheets that may be reproduced are included. One provides a sample of a fable and the suggestion that the student use it as a model to write his own. The other sheet contains suggestions for research that may be done by an individual or a group.

## » ANDROCLESE AND THE LION

Androcles (an' drō klēz) was a Roman slave who was mistreated by his master. Androcles ran away and hid in a cave to get away from cruelties. While Androcles was in the cave, a lion entered and held up his swollen paw. "Why, you have a big sliver in your paw," said Androcles. "No wonder your paw is swollen. Hold still and I will take out the sliver."

So Androcles took out the sliver. Then the lion gratefully licked the hand of Androcles and left.

A short time later soldiers came to the cave and found Androcles. They took him to Rome and threw him to a lion while hundreds of spectators watched.

Of course everyone expected the lion to tear Androcles to shreds but the lion only licked him. The people cheered. They held up their thumbs.

"Free him! Free him!" they yelled.

Androcles was freed. No longer was he a slave. By his kindness to a wounded creature, Androcles had lost his chains.

This story is a fable. A fable is a very short story that teaches a lesson. Aesopwas the most famous fable writer.

On the back of this paper, try writing one or more fables about subjects that come up in modern life. Show your fable to your teacher. Find out if you really wrote a fable or another kind of story.

What lesson does the story of "Androcles and the Lion" teach us? Do most fablehave human characters?

The class can be divided into groups which will read about the wonders of the world. Each group can list things to tell and report to the class. Someone might like to report on the new wonders of the world or make a list of the wonders they would select. You will have to research these in encyclopedias, online, and other books. If you prefer, work alone on this assignment.

## » WONDERS OF THE WORLD

The Temple of Artemis at Ephesus - Erected in the fourth century B.C.

The Statue of Zeus - Made by Phidias in the fifth century B.C.

The Mausoleum at Halicarnassus - Built in the fourth century B.C. A marble tomb.

The Colossus of Rhodes - Built 280 B.C. to the sun god Helios. One hundred five feet (31.2 meters) high. Destroyed later.

The Lighthouse at Alexandria, Egypt - Two hundred feet (60.06 meters) high. Light at peak. Destroyed in the fourteenth century.

Some lists include the catacombs of Alexandria, which were used for refuge by the Christians.

# ANSWER KEYS

## SECTION 1

**1.1** Balkan

**1.2** mountains and valleys cut Greece into small sections

**1.3** harbors

**1.4** stony, dry

**1.5** along the eastern border

**1.6** They roamed or moved about.

**1.7** Example:
A very advanced civilization developed early.

**1.8** They would learn to write, to read, to farm, and to make crafts.

**1.9** in the 1800s

**1.10** climate

**1.11** a yellow dye

**1.12** Knossos

**1.13** huge jars

**1.14** Minotaur or the half-bull

**1.15** bull

**1.16** household protectors

**1.17** fish, birds, beef, barley, cheese, nuts, honey

**1.18** The Mycenaeans came from the southern part of the Balkan peninsula or Greece.

**1.19** time and effort

**1.20** project

**1.21** The Lion Gate

**1.22** Apollo and Poseidon

**1.23** woodcutter

**1.24** The Olympic Games united the city-states.

**1.25** People did not communicate with others outside their city-state.

**1.26** The modern Olympic Games are held every four years.

**1.27** Example:
All the countries of the world are invited to send athletes to the modern Olympics. In ancient Greece, all the city-states participated. Political differences are put aside during the games.

**1.28** d

**1.29** c

**1.30** e

**1.31** a

**1.32** b

**1.33** Do not accept gifts from your enemies.

**1.34** He attacked Troy.

**1.35** a. He established a supreme court.
b. He cancelled farmers' debts.
c. He put a limit on the amount of land that could be owned by nobles.
d. He started a system of coins.
e. He punished people who would not work.
f. He made all free men citizens.

**1.36** The Delian League united the city-states for protection.

**1.37** The Golden Age of Greece was a time of more participation in government by poor people. A court system with juries was started. Office holders were paid in order to keep down corruption

**1.38** Children had pets, played ball games, had races with little chariots pulled by dogs, made objects from scraps, learned poetry, music and dancing.

**1.39** eighteen

**1.40** The Greeks had helped Asia Minor.

**1.41** They had weapons of metal.

**1.42** He and a few men fought 30,000 Persians until they all died fighting.

**1.43** The Greeks were prepared.

**1.44** The Greeks let the Persians crowd in the bay. They could not maneuver.

**1.45** The plague, lack of food for Athens, destruction of the Athenian navy, and the Spartan training made it possible for Sparta to win the war.

**1.46** He died of the plague.

**1.47** Greece was weak from wars.

**1.48** He wanted to conquer the world. He did not succeed, but he conquered as much as he knew of it.

**1.49** War destroys the strongest young men. It weakens morale. Often, the greatest buildings, art, and churches are destroyed. Many people are crippled or starved.

**1.50** true

**1.51** true

**1.52** false

**1.53** false

**1.54** true

**1.55** true

**1.56** military state

**1.57** Cleisthenes

**1.58** Pericles

**1.59** the enjoyment of life

**1.60** serve in the army
**1.61** died by poison
**1.62** because he obeyed the laws
**1.63** a. spiritual
b. physical
**1.64** democratic government
**1.65** too much and too little
**1.66** There are countless ways in which we imitate the Greeks.
**1.67** a. Greeks held beauty contests and so do we.
b. Greek letters and symbols are used for honor societies.
**1.68** b. princess
c. poetess
d. hostess
e. stewardess
f. baroness
g. heiress
h. duchess

# SELF TEST 1

**1.01** c
**1.02** g
**1.03** a
**1.04** k
**1.05** d
**1.06** h
**1.07** i
**1.08** m
**1.09** b
**1.010** e
**1.011** Mediterranean
**1.012** mountains
**1.013** Hippocratic oath
**1.014** Sparta
**1.015** ships
**1.016** Athens
**1.017** history
**1.018** Socrates
**1.019** Sparta
**1.020** showing it
**1.021** father of democracy
**1.022** city-states of Greece
**1.023** Aristotle
**1.024** Crete
**1.025** Plato
**1.026** true
**1.027** false
**1.028** true
**1.029** true
**1.030** false
**1.031** true
**1.032** false
**1.033** true
**1.034** false
**1.035** true

# SECTION 2

**2.1** Tiber
**2.2** Italian
**2.3** Alps
**2.4** Apennines
**2.5** Sicily
**2.6** trading post
**2.7** The two classes of people were the plebeians and the patricians.
**2.8** The Twelve Tables were the written laws of Rome.
**2.9** He was the Carthage general who led his men and elephants across the Alps.
**2.10** They were greedy and cruel.
**2.11** Rome fought Carthage three times.
**2.12** c. the entire Mediterranean world
**2.13** a. city mob
**2.14** b. war profits
**2.15** b. new middle class
**2.16** There were too many war prisoners, slaves, and farmers without land who had no work.
**2.17** They built roads and bridges, collected taxes and lent money
**2.18** He was a slave who led a rebellion.
**2.19** They tried to reform the government of Rome.
**2.20** Example:
I think the land reform was most important
**2.21** Example:
He established a postal system, gave salaries to tax collectors, and punished dishonesty.
**2.22** false
**2.23** true
**2.24** false
**2.25** false
**2.26** true
**2.27** true
**2.28** false
**2.29** true
**2.30** true
**2.31** false
**2.32** false
**2.33** true
**2.34** true
**2.35** d

**2.36** e
**2.37** f
**2.38** c
**2.39** i
**2.40** h
**2.41** g
**2.42** b
**2.43** *Lives of Famous Men*
**2.44** aqueducts
**2.45** Justinian Code
**2.46** Latin
**2.47** Polybius
**2.48** a. the disappearance of money
b. the decline of trade
c. the control of government over economic welfare
d. the decrease in value of the coin
e. laws that bound people to the same jobs
**2.49** Work had become a mark of disgrace.
**2.50** Life had become cheap.
**2.51** a. al
b. ical
c. ry
d. ry
e. al
f. ry
g. al
h. ry
i. al
j. al
k. ical
l. ry
**2.52** Examples:
a. solemn, inspiring, majestic, breathtaking
b. unrefined, rough, harsh, scratchy, crude
c. risky, hazardous, dangerous, unsafe
d. inactive, unemployed, unoccupied, pointless
e. skinny, bony, lean, wasted, spare, rawboned
f. holder, receptacle, carton, box, vessel
g. dictator, slave driver, absolute ruler, bully
h. mislay, lose, lose track of

## SELF TEST 2

| | |
|---|---|
| **2.01** | in a strategic place |
| **2.02** | trading station |
| **2.03** | privileges |
| **2.04** | no rights |
| **2.05** | the written laws of Rome |
| **2.06** | king |
| **2.07** | farmers without land |
| **2.08** | the Mediterranean world |
| **2.09** | Punic Wars |
| **2.010** | Latin language |
| **2.011** | true |
| **2.012** | false |
| **2.013** | true |
| **2.014** | true |
| **2.015** | true |
| **2.016** | true |
| **2.017** | false |
| **2.018** | true |
| **2.019** | false |
| **2.020** | false |
| **2.021** | innocent until proven guilty |
| **2.022** | aqueducts |
| **2.023** | west central |
| **2.024** | Apennines |
| **2.025** | a social disgrace |

**2.026** Example:
Plato taught principles of democracy and reason. He stressed that the spiritual was more important than the physical. He wanted harmony and efficiency.

**2.027** Paul perceived the Athenians were too superstitious. He knew of the idol to "the unknown God" and the many other idols in Athens.

**2.028** The three classes of citizens were the: spartiates—rulers, Perioeci—allies, helots—lowest class.

**2.029** Greece is located in the lower Balkan peninsula bounded by the Aegean Sea and Adriatic Sea.

**2.030** Examples:
geometry, levees, pulleys, mathematics, medical instruments, philosophy, and architecture (any contribution)

| | |
|---|---|
| **2.031** | Socrates, hemlock |
| **2.032** | Alexander, conquered world |
| **2.033** | Euclid, geometry |
| **2.034** | military state, Sparta |
| **2.035** | Hannibal, elephants |

## LIFEPAC TEST

| | | |
|---|---|---|
| 1. | h | |
| 2. | m | |
| 3. | c | |
| 4. | g | |
| 5. | b | |
| 6. | e | |
| 7. | k | |
| 8. | l | |
| 9. | a | |
| 10. | i | |
| 11. | a. | an Epicurean |
| 12. | c. | Greece |
| 13. | b. | king |
| 14. | c. | crucifixion |
| 15. | b. | Greece |
| 16. | b. | put them out of business |
| 17. | c. | insufficient space |
| 18. | b. | Sparta |
| 19. | b. | gladiators |
| 20. | | Hippocratic oath |
| 21. | | she had weapons of metal |
| 22. | | questioned ideas |
| 23. | | was not a criminal |
| 24. | | winning |
| 25. | | Spartiates |
| 26. | | democracy |
| 27. | | Tiber River |

28. Examples:
languages, democracy, architecture, art, medicine, scientific discovery, development of intellectual thinking

29. Examples:
Latin language , network of roads, stability, laws, literature, bridges, aqueducts, states medicine

30. Examples:
inflation, distaste for work, economy based on war, poor farming methods, plagues, violence, dishonesty

31. Examples:
the language for recording the New Testament, the roads for easy travel, intellectual thinking to understand Christ's teachings, stability so people could concentrate on spiritual things

# ALTERNATE LIFEPAC TEST

1.   true
2.   false
3.   true
4.   true
5.   true
6.   true
7.   true
8.   false
9.   true
10.  true
11.  Latin language
12.  Persians
13.  Leonidas
14.  horse
15.  Greece
16.  tribunes
17.  aqueducts
18.  Parthenon
19.  freedoms
20.  mobs
21.  c.  crucifixion
22.  a.  Sparta
23.  a.  Sparta
24.  c.  Italy
25.  c.  Hippocrates
26.  a.  Marathon
27.  b.  columns
28.  a.  the Twelve Tables
29.  b.  reason
30.  c.  too much and too little
31.  g
32.  k
33.  b
34.  a
35.  i
36.  d
37.  e
38.  f
39.  j
40.  c

# HISTORY & GEOGRAPHY 603

## ALTERNATE LIFEPAC TEST

NAME _____

DATE _____

SCORE _____

**Write true or false** (each answer, 2 points).

1. _____ Two major city-states of ancient Greece were Sparta and Athens.

2. _____ Most of the Grecian soil was fertile.

3. _____ From the Greeks we were given the idea of a democratic form of government.

4. _____ The many struggles between Carthage and Rome were called the Punic Wars.

5. _____ During the decline, Romans thought work to be a social disgrace.

6. _____ The Cretan civilization was unearthed in 1870.

7. _____ The Cretans were captured by the Mycenaeans from Greece.

8. _____ Romans were always kind to their children.

9. _____ A great Greek sculptor was Phidias.

10. _____ In Greece the serfs, or low classes, were called helots.

**Write the correct answer from the list on each line** (each answer, 3 points).

| | | |
|---|---|---|
| crucifixion | Latin language | Persians |
| freedoms | Leonidas | tribunes |
| Greece | mobs | tunics |
| horse | Parthenon | aqueducts |

11. A great contribution of the Romans to our world was the _____ .

12. Too many ships in a small space lost the battle of Salamis for the _____ .

13. With only a few men, the pass at Thermopylae was held by a brave Spartan named _____

    _____ .

14. The battle of Troy was won with the help of a wooden _____ .

15. In 776 B.C. the Olympic Games started in _____ .

16. During the Republic two elected consuls who took the place of a king were

    called _____ .

17. Romans were famous for their bridges, roads, and _____ .

18. A classic example of Greek architecture is the _____ .

19. In Crete, women had many _____ .

20. In Rome, slaves and prisoners from wars began to form city _____ .

**Write the correct letter and answer on each line** (each answer, 2 points).

21. Although He had broken no laws, Jesus was illegally punished by _____ .
    a. beating          b. imprisonment          c. crucifixion

22. The city-state in which a boy of seven was taught to endure discomfort was

    _____ .
    a. Sparta          b. Athens          c. Rome

23. The Spartiates were the ruling people in _____ .
    a. Sparta          b. Athens          c. Rome

24. Rome was built on the boot-shaped land of _____ .
    a. the Iberian peninsula      b. Sicily          c. Italy

25. Doctors today still take the oath written by the Greek, _____ .
    a. Socrates          b. Euclid          c. Hippocrates

26. The famous battle in which a small number of Greeks won over many Persians because the

    Greeks had metal spears and swords was _____ .
    a. Marathon          b. Salamis          c. Athens

27. Greek architecture has many _____ .
    a. domes          b. columns          c. bricks

**28.** The code of laws for the first Roman republic was called _____ .
a. The Twelve Tables        b. The Ten Commandments    c. Justinian Code

**29.** Above all, Plato believed that men should be ruled by _____ .
a. the strong            b. reason            c. the brightest

**30.** Aristotle's Golden Mean meant a balance between _____ .
a. hot and cold          b. high and low          c. too much and too little

**Match these items** (each answer, 3 points).

**31.** _____ Knossos

**32.** _____ Troy

**33.** _____ snakes

**34.** _____ Socrates

**35.** _____ Spartiates

**36.** _____ elephants

**37.** _____ plebians

**38.** _____ dependence on war

**39.** _____ patricians

**40.** _____ New Testament

a. hemlock

b. Cretan protectors

c. Greek language

d. Hannibal

e. had no rights

f. downfall of Rome

g. Cretan capital

h. Sicily

i. ruling class in Sparta

j. had special privileges

k. Trojans

# HISTORY & GEOGRAPHY 604

Unit 4: Life in the Middle Ages

# TEACHING NOTES

| MATERIALS NEEDED FOR LIFEPAC | |
|---|---|
| Required | Suggested |
| (None) | • Bible<br>• dictionary<br>• globe<br>• (the reference materials can be either in book or online formats) |

### Section 1: The Feudal System

1. Map study—Look at a map of the Western Roman Empire before it fell to the barbarians. Compare the same territory after the conquest. Point out that the change came gradually. Barbarians filtered into the empire for a century before Rome finally fell. For many decades the areas of central Europe and elsewhere were still referred to as the Roman Empire though it was actually barbarian territory. Mention Charlemagne.

2. Have students name some ancestors of theirs who were, in fact, barbarians English, French, German (anyone who was not Roman or Greek.)

3. Compare the stability of the Roman Catholic Church to the instability of the Roman Empire.

4. Look up one more of these stories. Each classmate takes one. When you read the stories, tell each other. Then act out the stories for the classroom.

    - Sir Galahad and the Holy Grail (English)

    - King Arthur and the Knights of the Round Table (English)

    - Beowulf (Denmark)

    - Cid (Spain)

    - Alfred the Great (Saxon)

    - Songs of Roland (France)

    - Robin Hood (English). After reading about the system of land ownership, do you have a better idea of the kind of "outlaw" Robin Hood was?

5. Make a model or detailed colored picture of one of these. Use other references as well as your LIFEPAC.

    - Castle, moat, and barriers

    - Manor and grounds

    - Villein's hut, inside and out

## Section 2: The Daily Life

1. Discuss with the students the meaning of real poverty. Do we know anything like the poverty of the serfs or even the villeins of that day?

2. Discuss the disease epidemics of the Middle Ages, the Black Death (Bubonic plague), even smallpox. Ask if they understand the word *quarantine*. Under what circumstances do we hear the word today? (More often with sick cattle, etc.)

3. Look up medicines of the Middle Ages. For fun, pretend a classmate is sick. Treat him with (pretend) medicines such as used in the Dark Ages. You and your classmate will have to do some research. Ask your librarian (either school or public) to help you. Look up the word *alchemy*.

4. Choose one of these projects and do a good job of showing to your teacher or class what you have done. You will have to research these.

    a. Describe the parts of a suit of armor.

    b. Draw or make a model of a lady of the Middle Ages. Be sure you have all the parts of her clothing, such as hats or other hair covering, dresses, cloaks, and shoes.

    c. Draw a king, lord, or knight. Put on him the important pieces of clothing.

## Section 3: Books and Schools

1. Discuss with students the difference between schools today and those of the Middle Ages. Schools are often started in churches for various reasons. What are some of these reasons? Are the reasons different for a school starting today and the ones that started in the Middle Ages?

2. Pretend a classmate cannot write and you can. Write a letter for him, preferably on paper that has been wet and let dry, so that it will look more like parchment. Be sure to try to write as a scribe would have, and the subject should be a Middle Ages subject. Seal it as it would have been sealed then.

3. On a piece of very good paper, (construction paper will suffice), print as well as you can one of your favorite Psalms. Do the printing in the very center of your paper. Make the first letter large with color and swirls of gold. Around the edge of the Psalm make flowers like vines with leaves and perhaps an angel cherub or two. This sheet will remind you of books called Psalters (books of Psalms) printed by hand by the early monks in monasteries. Make more than one and put them together to make your own Psalter. If you prefer, transfer your writing and designs to a nice piece of cloth. Then embroider the writing and design. Hang it in your room at home or at school.

## Section 4: Islam

1. Collect pictures of Islamic art and architecture from old magazines or online sources. Make a collage out of them. Discuss how it is different from Christian art and architecture.

2. Invite some one who has lived in a Muslim country (missionary, military officer, etc.) to speak to your class. Ask them about how Islam affects the culture of the country.

3. At the library or online, research how women are treated in a Muslim country. Present the information to the class and discuss it.

4. Obtain a library book (or books) on the military expansion of Islam during the time frame covered in the LIFEPAC. Make a copy of a map of Europe, North Africa, and western Asia. Color in all of the areas conquered by the Muslim armies. Put in the dates the important cities were conquered (i.e. Alexandria, Constantinople, Baghdad, etc.). If the city was later liberated from Muslim rule, write in that date as well. Put up the map on the classroom wall.

### Section 5: The Crusades

1. Discuss with the students the reasons for the Crusades and what they did or did not accomplish.

2. Help the students to understand the reasons for the Children's Crusade. Is there anything in our day to compare with it? If not, what makes the difference between our day and the Middle Ages?

3. Make a corner of the classroom a place for Hospitalers to aid the sick. Act it out.

4. Make up a short play about children on the Crusade and the capture of them by slaveholders. Discuss what happened to the children and why they may have wanted to go on the Crusade in the first place.

### Section 6: The Trade System

1. Be sure the student understands the meaning of guilds, apprentice, journeyman, and master. With students, compare the unions of today and the guilds of the Middle Ages.

2. If you have enough students, stage your own fair. Half can be merchants, the other half buyers. Set up the fair as described in your LIFEPAC. Make streets called Baker Street, Glass Street, and so forth. Paint a background showing a cathedral and a castle. Be sure some of you dress as jugglers, minstrels, and all of the other people mentioned as going to a fair in your LIFEPAC.

3. Make a festive poster about a fair. Include drawings or pictures of all the people at the fair mentioned in the LIFEPAC. Be sure to include a knight, a nobleman, his family, and attendants.

### Section 7: The Cathedrals

1. Be sure the student understands that the Roman Catholic Church kept Christianity alive in the Middle Ages. There were no other churches. Although the church was eventually corrupted by power, out from it would come such men as Martin Luther, John Calvin, and others, who would lead men back into the truth of God's Word.

2. Write a play (drama) to depict the holiday you are nearest to celebrating (Thanksgiving, Christmas, Easter). Try to make this play like the liturgical drama of the Middle Ages churches. You may have to do some reading about church dramas. Act out your play for the classroom.

3. Stained glass windows can be made very easily. Read about the subject as much as you can. The shape of your window can be round or oblong. Each student makes a design the size that has been agreed upon. The outlines of the design are traced on black construction paper. The black paper represents the lead frame in real windows. The parts that represent glass are cut out and filled in with colored tissue paper. If rich colors are desired, two sheets of tissue are better. You may have someone make a frame for your windows. Sometimes these windows are displayed in the classroom window.

# STUDENT WORKSHEET

The following activity may be reproduced as a student worksheet that involves both research and art work.

Here are some pictures of shields used by knights and kings.

If you wish, look up the parts of the shield. What symbols did shields carry?

Different emblems signified important things. Find out about them. Make a display and report.

Find out all about knights. How did knighthood begin? Ask your librarian to help you.

Research warfare in the days of knights. Who fought whom? How were their horses dressed?

What weapons did they use? Make a poster display of pictures you draw or find in old magazines.

Here is a picture of a young boy who might have gone on the Children's Crusade.

If he were a crusader, what would the insignia on the front of his shirt be?

How old was a boy before he was taught the skills of warfare?

Research these questions. Then copy this picture. Label the different parts of his dress and equipment.

If he crusaded, would he have worn anything on his head?

Look up this information. Show your picture and give a talk to the class.

## » RESEARCH NOTES

# ANSWER KEYS

## SECTION 1

| | |
|---|---|
| **1.1** | b |
| **1.2** | a |
| **1.3** | b |
| **1.4** | b |
| **1.5** | a |
| **1.6-1.12** | Any seven of the following ten tribes; any order:<br>Anglo Saxons, Celts, Franks, Slavs, Burgundians, Ostrogoths, Visigoths, Suevi, Vandals, Moors |
| **1.13** | learning |
| **1.14** | Middle Ages |
| **1.15** | Example:<br>Law and order began to appear after years of barbaric violence. |
| **1.16** | Example:<br>People were grouped in classes: some people were even serfs or slaves. |
| **1.17** | land gifts called manors |
| **1.18** | vassals |
| **1.19** | feudal system |
| **1.20** | products and services |
| **1.21** | protection, peace, and security |
| **1.22** | a. live in a town undetected for a year and a day<br>b. enter the service of the Catholic church<br>c. join a band of outlaws |
| **1.23** | false |
| **1.24** | false |
| **1.25** | true |
| **1.26** | false |
| **1.27** | true |
| **1.28** | Teacher check |

## SELF TEST 1

| | |
|---|---|
| **1.01** | vassals or serfs |
| **1.02** | lords or nobles |
| **1.03** | feudalism |
| **1.04** | serfs |
| **1.05** | protection |
| **1.06** | manors |
| **1.07** | the king, usually |
| **1.08** | The villeins were very poor people who worked for the lord or the town. |
| **1.09** | The lord could move to another manor which he owned. |
| **1.010** | Example:<br>A villein could flee to a town and remain a year and a day without being caught. |
| **1.011** | false |
| **1.012** | true |
| **1.013** | true |
| **1.014** | false |
| **1.015** | true |
| **1.016** | true |
| **1.017** | true |
| **1.018** | false |
| **1.019** | false |
| **1.020** | true |
| **1.021** | Any four of the following:<br>Franks, Angles, Saxon, Celts, Moors, Burgundians, Suevi, Vandals, Visigoths |
| **1.022** | Rome had become morally weak. Rome was poor spiritually. |
| **1.023** | Under the feudal system, people paid their taxes in products and in services. |
| **1.024** | The barbarians brought violence and destruction everywhere they went. People lived in ignorance and danger. |
| **1.025** | Each manor had its own pasture lands, mill, wine press, church, and village. |
| **1.026** | f |
| **1.027** | g |
| **1.028** | h |
| **1.029** | a |
| **1.030** | i |
| **1.031** | j |
| **1.032** | c |
| **1.033** | b |
| **1.034** | d |
| **1.035** | e |

# SECTION 2

| | |
|---|---|
| **2.1** | pumice stone |
| **2.2** | they were covered with dirt |
| **2.3** | chest |
| **2.4** | canopies |
| **2.5** | there were few lights and the clocks were unreliable |
| **2.6** | once a week |
| **2.7** | people retired early |
| **2.8** | bedside |
| **2.9** | togas |
| **2.10** | Crusades |
| **2.11** | trousers or tunic |
| **2.12** | full and long |
| **2.13** | Example: More meat and fewer vegetables and fruits were eaten. |
| **2.14** | Example: The water was very polluted and probably tasted bad. |

**2.15** Either order:
a. upper class
b. lower class

**2.16** a. ginger
b. cloves
c. pepper
d. nutmeg
e. cinnamon

**2.17** away, or apart
**2.18** pages
**2.19** carvers

**2.20** a. swans
b. peacocks
c. partridges

**2.21** a. ale
b. wine
c. apple cider
d. milk

**2.22** Teacher check
**2.23** b. an outdoor toilet
**2.24** c. open fires
**2.25** a. thieves could enter easily
**2.26** b. system of pipes

**2.27** The roots are
a. market
b. wonder
c. adequate
d. possible
e. prune
f. cherish
g. confess
h. aristocrat
i. noble
j. knight
k. port
l. proceed
m. attack
n. ceremony

**2.28** Example: Cities had plagues because of filth, no health laws, superstitions and ignorance.

**2.29** Example: We practice cleanliness and we have antibiotics to cure diseases.

**2.30** Venice
**2.31** Teacher check
**2.32** I would excuse no one.
**2.33** Teacher check

**2.34** a. Castilian
b. Spanish
c. Roman
d. Western
e. Biblical
f. of or pertaining to Castile
g. belonging to Spain
h. of or pertaining to Rome
i. belonging to the West
j. pertaining to the Bible

**2.35** a. Benedict
b. Benedictine
c. Benedictinism
d. benediction
e. benedictional
f. benedictionary
g. benefaction
h. benefactress
i. beneficial
j. beneficiary

# SELF TEST 2

| | |
|---|---|
| **2.01** | A.D. 400-1500 |
| **2.02** | the barbarians |
| **2.03** | lost |
| **2.04** | lords and nobles |
| **2.05** | legends |
| **2.06** | lord |
| **2.07** | villeins |
| **2.08** | in isolation |
| **2.09** | a year and a day |
| **2.010** | no |
| **2.011** | drawbridge |
| **2.012** | protection |
| **2.013** | moats |
| **2.014** | dirt |
| **2.015** | mutton fat |
| **2.016** | manors |
| **2.017** | smallpox, diphtheria, tetanus, influenza, leprosy |
| **2.018** | no (explanations will vary) |
| **2.019** | Rotting garbage makes good breeding ground for flies and other insects that spreads germs. |
| **2.020** | h. protection |
| **2.021** | f. main item on dining table |
| **2.022** | g. man's shirt |
| **2.023** | b. movable grating |
| **2.024** | j. isolation |
| **2.025** | c. shaving |
| **2.026** | i. tell time |
| **2.027** | a. bed |
| **2.028** | d. spoilage of meat |
| **2.029** | e. kitchen help |
| **2.030** | false |
| **2.031** | true |
| **2.032** | true |
| **2.033** | true |
| **2.034** | true |
| **2.035** | true |
| **2.036** | false |
| **2.037** | true |
| **2.038** | false |

# SECTION 3

| | |
|---|---|
| **3.1** | quills or reeds |
| **3.2** | plants and minerals |
| **3.3** | a. skin <br> b. animals |
| **3.4** | scraping with something sharp |
| **3.5** | scribes |
| **3.6** | messengers |
| **3.7** | Latin |
| **3.8** | religion and current events |
| **3.9** | He could write something different. He would learn your business. |
| **3.10** | They could not attend school. |
| **3.11** | Teacher check |
| **3.12** | Teacher check |
| **3.13** | The first Catholic schools were started to educate choir boys. |
| **3.14** | One of the most important schools was Jarrow. |
| **3.15** | Bede was a teacher at Jarrow who wrote a famous history of England. |
| **3.16** | The subjects girls learned are contrasted as follows: then–homemaking arts, music, occasionally to read and write; now–academic subjects and sometimes homemaking arts |
| **3.17** | Teacher check |
| **3.18** | Children were whipped to prove an instructor's ability to teach. The instructors thought whippings drove out Satan from the students. Children were also flogged to remind them of others who had suffered. |
| **3.19** | Children were whipped in memory of the children killed by Herod. |
| **3.20** | His former students cared for the elderly schoolmaster. |
| **3.21** | King Alfred |
| **3.22** | Charlemagne |
| **3.23** | Roman numerals |
| **3.24** | He wanted people to be able to improve their lives. |
| **3.25** | false |
| **3.26** | false |
| **3.27** | true |
| **3.28** | true |
| **3.29** | Benediction means the oral saying of a blessing or prayer. |
| **3.30** | It is usually heard at the end of a religious service. |
| **3.31** | fame ous |
| **3.32** | erase able |
| **3.33** | monasteries |
| **3.34** | histories |

| | |
|---|---|
| **3.35** | victories |
| **3.36** | centuries |
| **3.37** | granaries |
| **3.38** | tries |
| **3.39** | ladies |

# SELF TEST 3

**3.01**    a. quills
**3.02**    b. plants and minerals
**3.03**    b. bladders of animals
**3.04**    a. schoolmaster
**3.05**    a. could not read or write
**3.06**    b. law
**3.07**    b. medicine
**3.08**    a. pipe organ
**3.09**    b. no postal system
**3.010**    b. to drive out Satan
**3.011**    Example answers:
books, televisions, automobiles, buses, letters, prescriptions for medicine.
**3.012**    The books took so long to write and few could read.
**3.013**    Religious materials and current event stories were written.
**3.014**    Latin was read in all countries.
**3.015**    The Library of Congress is our country's largest library.
**3.016**    Children were whipped to prove an instructor's ability to teach. Children were whipped to drive out Satan's evil spirit. Children were also whipped to remind them of others who had suffered.
**3.017**    A legend is a popular story handed down from earlier times.
**3.018**    He insisted that the clergy learn to write correctly. He wanted learning for all.
**3.019**    true
**3.020**    true
**3.021**    false
**3.022**    true
**3.023**    true
**3.024**    false
**3.025**    true
**3.026**    true
**3.027**    false
**3.028**    false

# SECTION 4

| | |
|---|---|
| **4.1** | false |
| **4.2** | true |
| **4.3** | true |
| **4.4** | false |
| **4.5** | false |
| **4.6** | If the Muslims had won they would have been free to conquer Europe and spread Islam there. |
| **4.7** | by war |
| **4.8** | They believed if they died fighting for Islam they would go straight to heaven. |
| **4.9** | Islam's holy book; believed to be the words the Angel Gabriel spoke to Muhammad |
| **4.10** | a holy war |
| **4.11** | the Angel Gabriel |
| **4.12** | over 700 years |
| **4.13** | Muhammad |
| **4.14** | successor |
| **4.15** | Ka'bah |
| **4.16** | Arabic numbers, algebra, paper |
| **4.17** | 1. Pray five times a day |
| | 2. Believe there is only one god and Muhammad is his prophet |
| | 3. Fast during daylight in the ninth month |
| | 4. Give alms to the poor |
| | 5. Pilgrimage to Mecca |
| **4.18** | a prophet |
| **4.19** | Taj Mahal |
| **4.20** | people, plants, or animals |
| **4.21** | Europe |
| **4.22** | people of the book |
| **4.23** | mosque |
| **4.24** | abstract |
| **4.25** | true |
| **4.26** | false |
| **4.27** | false |
| **4.28** | false |
| **4.29** | true |
| **4.30** | Teacher check |

# SELF TEST 4

| | |
|---|---|
| **4.01** | caliph |
| **4.02** | Ka'bah |
| **4.03** | Mecca |
| **4.04** | prophet |
| **4.05** | jihad |
| **4.06** | mosque |
| **4.07** | calligraphy |
| **4.08** | Koran |
| **4.09** | algebra |
| **4.010** | abstract |
| **4.011** | blank |
| **4.012** | X |
| **4.013** | X |
| **4.014** | blank |
| **4.015** | X |
| **4.016** | X |
| **4.017** | blank |
| **4.018** | blank |
| **4.019** | blank |
| **4.020** | X |
| **4.021** | false |
| **4.022** | false |
| **4.023** | true |
| **4.024** | true |
| **4.025** | false |
| **4.026** | true |
| **4.027** | true |
| **4.028** | false |
| **4.029** | false |
| **4.030** | false |
| **4.031** | people of the book |
| **4.032** | Taj Mahal |
| **4.033** | prophet |
| **4.034** | Turkey, Spain, India, Iran, or Egypt |
| **4.035** | works |
| **4.036** | Muhammad taught that a man who died fighting for Islam went straight to heaven. Therefore, the men fought hard and well. |
| **4.037** | The Muslims fought Charles Martel at Poitiers. This battle stopped the Muslim advance and protected Christian Europe. |
| **4.038** | Muslims believe that Muhammad was the last and the greatest of the prophets. He was the only prophet to receive all of God's word correctly. |

# SECTION 5

| | | | | |
|---|---|---|---|---|
| **5.1** | true | | **5.26** | aided Muslim |
| **5.2** | true | | **5.27** | gentle ways |
| **5.3** | true | | **5.28** | They began to fight against their enemies. |

**5.1** true
**5.2** true
**5.3** true
**5.4** true
**5.5** rules
**5.6** substitute
**5.7** armed guard
**5.8** proof
**5.9** The Muslims won.
**5.10** He was a boy who led 20,000 children on a Crusade.
**5.11** He was a boy who led 30,000 children on a Crusade.
**5.12** They died or were sold as slaves.
**5.13** They cared for the sick Crusaders.
**5.14** Those who belonged to the Order of the Holy Trinity sometimes offered themselves in exchange for the captives.
**5.15** The Benedictines were scholarly monks.
**5.16** These groups were important because many Crusaders needed help. Many were ignorant, ill, or mistreated.
**5.17** No, some people treated the Christians kindly.
**5.18** Haroun al Raschid treated the Christians kindly.
**5.19** First
**5.20** c. is cruel to others
**5.21** Teacher check
**5.22** Teacher check
**5.23** Teacher check
**5.24** tolerant
**5.25** ideas, products

**5.26** aided Muslim
**5.27** gentle ways
**5.28** They began to fight against their enemies. They began to attack nonbelievers or heretics and the peasants in Germany.
**5.29** Teacher check
**5.30** a. we're
b. they've
c. you're
d. I'm
e. they're
f. I'll
g. don't
h. wasn't
i. aren't
j. didn't
**5.31** a. 9
b. 10
c. 7
d. 8
e. 3
f. 4
g. 6
h. 1
i. 2
j. 5
**5.32** a. not tolerant
b. not decent
c. write again
d. set again
e. go toward
f. a change toward the correct way

# SELF TEST 5

**5.01** faith in God and leaders
**5.02** Crusades
**5.03** to take it from the Muslims
**5.04** yes
**5.05** vow
**5.06** his son or substitute
**5.07** children were shipped as slaves
**5.08** thousands
**5.09** b. our enemies
**5.010** yes
**5.011** sick crusaders
**5.012** Muslim or Muhammadan
**5.013** kindly
**5.014** They began to fight against peasants in Germany and to attack nonbelievers and heretics.
**5.015** The Crusades enriched people with new ideas, new fabrics, and more tolerance.
**5.016** They would be helpful. They were hardy and used to hard labor. They could do many tasks.
**5.017** All Muslims were not cruel to Crusaders. At least one Arab, Haroun al Raschid, was kind.
**5.018** false
**5.019** true
**5.020** false
**5.021** true
**5.022** true
**5.023** false
**5.024** true
**5.025** true
**5.026** false
**5.027** true
**5.028** cruel
**5.029** English
**5.030** thatch
**5.031** peace
**5.032** quarantine law

# SECTION 6

**6.1** castles
**6.2** Example:
busy places, near churches, near rivers, near important roads, monasteries
**6.3** Lords wanted to carry on Crusades or wars.
**6.4** They wanted charters of freedom so that they could manage their own affairs.
**6.5** People had seen new treasures during Crusades to foreign lands.
**6.6** Merchants wanted to sell beautiful things
**6.7** The use of money replaced the exchanging of goods.
**6.8** They could buy lands with money.
**6.9** Merchants took orders from customers
**6.10** They would live on Baker Street.
**6.11** guild
**6.12** apprenticeship
**6.13** journeyman
**6.14** master
**6.15** He was fined or punished.
**6.16** true
**6.17** false
**6.18** true
**6.19** true
**6.20** Jugglers, singers, dancers, speakers, and guitar players provided entertainment.
**6.21** Wandering minstrels and beggars brought news from other lands.
**6.22** Knights or nobles rode through the town.
**6.23** Yes, we have fairs in the fall for all kinds of products. We also have art fairs and display fairs in big convention centers.
**6.24** fairs
**6.25** All kinds or products were sold. Also produce from farms and luxuries from other lands were sold.
**6.26** None of the goods had prices.
**6.27** argue or haggle

# SELF TEST 6

**6.01** The barbarians destroyed works of art and burned books. Some art was lost for good.

**6.02** Monks wrote most of the books and started schools.

**6.03** Diseases spread rapidly because of lack of sanitation and ignorance of germs, poor plumbing, no refrigeration for foods, dirt, garbage, toilets in the floor.

**6.04** People had seen the beautiful items in foreign lands while on the Crusades.

**6.05** The merchant class was the new and powerful class.

**6.06** Money was easier to use was in demand.

**6.07** He would go during the fairs.

**6.08** Minstrels were singers who traveled with an instrument and sang stories.

**6.09** Merchants started guilds to set up rules and prices for products and services.

**6.010** At first, the shops were around the castles.

**6.011** The merchant class brought money and people to the towns. Trade was centralized in the towns.

**6.012** They had money and could buy the land when nobles were in need of money.

**6.013** Jews could not belong to a guild.

**6.014** moneylenders, financiers

**6.015** a. an apprentice
b. a journeyman

**6.016** true

**6.017** false

**6.018** false

**6.019** false

**6.020** false

**6.021** charters

**6.022** unions

**6.023** interest

**6.024** money

**6.025** fair

**6.026** bargain, argue about the price until agreement is reached

**6.027** the second step in learning a trade

**6.028** color used in paint

**6.029** the first step in learning a trade

**6.030** a person who deals with money

# SECTION 7

**7.1** hovels

**7.2** centers of life

**7.3** rise to high positions

**7.4** inspired

**7.5** b. taxes

**7.6** b. vassals

**7.7** b. punishment

**7.8** b. heaven

**7.9** They took years, often more than a century, to build.

**7.10** The art of making stained glass windows was perfected.

**7.11** Window glass was made from sand, salt, and ashes.

**7.12** They are removed and stored.

**7.13** Drama developed in the church to make messages clear.

**7.14** The priests were the first actors.

**7.15** It had the shape of a cross.

**7.16** The church has not always approved of drama.

**7.17** miracle play

**7.18** liturgical drama

**7.19** morality play

**7.20** mystery

**7.21** a. church
b. time-period
c. destroy
d. labor
e. stimulate
f. splendid
g. supernatural
h. unknown
i. aim
j. nonreligious

**7.22** a. wives
b. lives
c. leaves
d. loaves

**7.23** a. authorities
b. entities
c. granaries
d. holies
e. plays
f. pulleys

# SELF TEST 7

**7.01** barbarians
**7.02** 400 years
**7.03** monks
**7.04** fiefs
**7.05** produce
**7.06** eight feet thick
**7.07** meat
**7.08** seven years
**7.09** fork
**7.010** dried, scraped animal skins
**7.011** false
**7.012** false
**7.013** true
**7.014** false
**7.015** true
**7.016** merchant class
**7.017** fairs
**7.018** stories and news
**7.019** guilds
**7.020** cross
**7.021** money
**7.022** center
**7.023** bishopric
**7.024** sermon in Latin

**7.025** stained glass
**7.026** century
**7.027** Hospitalers
**7.028** Richard, the Lion-Hearted
**7.029** manor
**7.030** Venice
**7.031** Example:
People were grouped in different social classes. Some were thought to be better than other people.
**7.032** Example:
The monk scribes worked hard copying many books. They copied Bibles and prayers. They wrote records and current events of the day.
**7.033** Example:
People learned to be more tolerant of others. People became aware of different cultures. They discovered beautiful products from other places.
**7.034** Example:
The cathedrals reached toward the sky, and their spires inspired the lowly people in their daily tasks.

# LIFEPAC TEST

| | |
|---|---|
| I. | Rome |
| 2. | barbarians |
| 3. | protection |
| 4. | monks |
| 5. | cross |
| 6. | feudalism |
| 7. | fair |
| 8. | Crusades |
| 9. | monasteries |
| 10. | plague |
| 11. | true |
| 12. | false |
| 13. | false |
| 14. | true |
| 15. | true |
| 16. | true |
| 17. | false |
| 18. | false |
| 19. | nobles |
| 20. | Muhammad |
| 21. | could not belong to guilds |
| 22. | protection |
| 23. | sports ( or war games) |
| 24. | Crusades |
| 25. | scribes |
| 26. | free or independent |
| 27. | love |
| 28. | God |
| 29. | c. stained glass |
| 30. | c. authority |
| 31. | The best characteristic of the feudal system was the protection, peace, and security provided by the manor lord. This arrangement gave Europe a kind of stability. |
| 32. | The worst characteristic of the feudal system was that it was a fixed class society. If you were born a serf, you could not become a noble. You could not even leave the manor lands without permission from the lord of the manor. |
| **Note:** | the above answers for 31 and 32 are examples. Other good answers are possible and acceptable as long as the student can properly defend his or her answer from the text. |

# ALTERNATE LIFEPAC TEST

| | |
|---|---|
| I. | true |
| 2. | true |
| 3. | true |
| 4. | true |
| 5. | true |
| 6. | false |
| 7. | true |
| 8. | false |
| 9. | false |
| 10. | true |
| 11. | God |
| 12. | guilds |
| 13. | spices |
| 14. | manors |
| 15. | money |
| 16. | villeins |
| 17. | drama |
| 18. | smallpox |
| 19. | safety |
| 20. | slaves |
| 21. | money-lenders |
| 22. | recreation |
| 23. | pipe organ |
| 24. | crusades |
| 25. | drama |
| 26. | c. money |
| 27. | c. not perfected |
| 28. | c. lack of freedom |
| 29. | a. peace and protection |
| 30. | b. year |
| 31. | a. vassals |
| 32. | b. towns |
| 33. | f |
| 34. | e |
| 35. | h |
| 36. | c |
| 37. | g |
| 38. | d |
| 39. | a |

# HISTORY & GEOGRAPHY 604

## ALTERNATE LIFEPAC TEST

NAME  _____

DATE  _____

SCORE  _____

80
100

**Answer true or false** (each answer, 1 point).

1.  _____  The Romans ruled the Western World before the barbarian invasion.

2.  _____  The yearly fairs were joyful occasions.

3.  _____  The Goths and Franks were barbarians.

4.  _____  The crusades were journeys to capture the Holy Land.

5.  _____  A plague was a disease that could kill all the people of entire cities.

6.  _____  Churches were built in the shape of triangles.

7.  _____  Islam was founded by Muhammad.

8.  _____  Vassals worked for lords but received nothing in return.

9.  _____  During the Middle Ages there were no schools.

10.  _____  Feudalism was a system of land ownership.

**Write the correct answer from the list on each line** (each answer, 3 points).

| | | |
|---|---|---|
| drama | manors | smallpox |
| taxes | God | money |
| spices | villeins | guilds |

11. People who lived during the Middle Ages had faith in _____ .

12. To help establish rules of trade, merchants formed _____ .

13. To hide the spoilage of meat, cooks added _____ .

14. Independent communities were the _____ .

15. Trade developed better with _____ .

16. Poor people were the _____ .

17. Churches began the first _____ .

18. A severe disease that has almost disappeared today, but was common in the Middle Ages, was _____ .

**Unscramble the word and write it on the line** (each answer, 4 points).

19. _____  In time of attack, villagers hurried to the castles for yteasf.

20. _____  Children of the crusades were often sold as seaslv.

21. _____  Because Jews could not belong to the guilds, they became yeomn-sedelnr.

22. _____  Men especially liked hunting, archery, and javelin throwing for notecrerai.

23. _____  One of the musical instruments taught in early was the universities eipp gorna.

24. _____  After they returned from the sascrude, people wanted more luxuries.

25. _____  Houses of God were built with care, and madar was used in their services.

**Write the correct letter and answer on each line** (each answer, 2 points).

26. After the Crusades, instead of bartering, people began to buy with _____ .
    a. credit cards          b. farm products          c. money

27. Up until the Middle Ages, stained glass had not been used much in churches because it was
    _____ .
    a. not liked             b. expensive              c. not perfected

28. Probably the worst characteristic of feudalism was the _____ .
    a. cold castle           b. lack of schooling      c. lack of freedom

29. Probably the best characteristic of feudalism was the _____ .
    a. peace and protection  b. knighthood             c. health care

30. To have trade and entertainment, people had fairs every _____ .
    a. five years            b. year                   c. month

31. The nobles, or lords, gave land to _____ .
    a. vassals               b. serfs                  c. villeins

32. The nobles sold charters of freedom to _____ .
    a. prisoners             b. towns                  c. merchants

**Match these items** (each answer, 2 points).

33. _____ not on the table              a.  villein
34. _____ instead of paper              b.  castle
35. _____ giving alms                   c.  cared for the sick
36. _____ Hospitalers                   d.  Islam's holy book
37. _____ master, journey man           e.  dried animal skins
38. _____ Koran                         f.  fork
39. _____ thatched hut                  g.  craftsmen
                                          h.  pillar of Islam

# HISTORY & GEOGRAPHY 605

## Unit 5: Six South American Countries

# TEACHING NOTES

| MATERIALS NEEDED FOR LIFEPAC | |
| --- | --- |
| Required | Suggested |
| (None) | • atlas<br>• dictionary<br>• encyclopedia<br>• map of physical terrain of South America<br>• maps of transportation, vegetation zones, weather, and industries in South America<br>• (the reference materials can be either in book or online formats) |

## ADDITIONAL LEARNING ACTIVITIES

**Section 1: Brazil**

1.  Review with the students several kinds of maps of South America: physical, weather, rainfall, vegetation, and so forth.

2.  Review maps of Brazil with the students, especially physical maps that will show divisions of regions as mentioned in this LIFEPAC.

3.  Discuss with the students the work of the Protestant missionaries in South America, especially Brazil.

4.  With your classmates decide on a part of South America you like--the jungle, a city, rain forests, the Amazon River banks, anywhere. Make over a corner or other space in your classroom to depict your choice of location. For instance, if you choose the jungle, try to make a good jungle, including trees, bushes, wildflowers, birds, animals, snakes and a jungle village (or at least a house). Be sure you know if you have a Bush Negro or Indian village. Use materials you have at hand or can bring from home. When you are finished, explain your project to other students.

5.  Make posters of cities of Brazil, mentioning major reasons these cities are famous.

6.  Either draw or make a model of the city of Brasilia. This city was planned before it was ever built, and it follows a definite design.

7.  Start a scrapbook of pictures of wildlife and wildflowers found in Brazil. You may cut pictures from old magazines, find pictures in books and magazines, or online that you can copy and color in your own way. Be sure to label your pictures clearly. If the animal or flower has significance, include this fact on the page of your picture. When your pictures are organized, show and explain your scrapbook to someone. You might want to add to this scrapbook when you study the other countries of South America.

8.  Consult with your minister or returned missionary or a woman's worker in your church. Find out how many different kinds of missionaries serve in Brazil and other parts of South America. Make a list of the kinds of work they do, such as airplane pilot, translator, teacher, preacher, or doctor. Choose from this list one thing you would like to do if you were called to be a missionary to Brazil. On a separate piece of paper, write why you would choose this work. When you are finished, show this paper to your teacher.

9. Start a scrapbook or poster of flags of South America. Begin with the flag of Brazil. Either cut a picture from an old magazine, or, better yet, copy the flag and color it correctly yourself. Pictures of flags can be found in most encyclopedias or easily online.

## Section 2: Columbia

1. Go over the map of Colombia with the students. Integrate it with the map of total South America. Be sure to point out the three mountain ranges with valleys in between.

2. Give another classmate these directions:

   a. How to get from Cartagena to Medellin.

   b. How to get to Bogotá from Medellin.

   c. How to reach Santa Marta from Tumaco.

3. Make squares, about 25 inches on each side, of crepe paper. You may use old sheets or curtains if you prefer. Cut a hole in the exact middle of each one to put a head through. Make at least two, one for yourself and one for a classmate. You now have a sort of ruana. You and your friend may wear them as they are or decorate them.

4. Make a model of an Avianca Airlines plane or make a poster about Avianca Airlines travel. You may be able to get information from your local airport or online.

5. Make a picture of the Colombian flag. Add it to your collection.

6. If you wish, add Colombian plants and wildlife to your wildlife scrapbook started in the study of Brazil.

## Section 3: Venezuela and the Three Guianas

1. Go over the maps of Venezuela and the three Guianas with the students. Especially point out the terrain and physical aspects of the countries. Make sure the students know the location of Lake Maracaibo in Venezuela.

2. Discuss with the students possible physical reasons for the formation of the land and the use of it, or historical reasons why Venezuela remained under dictatorships for 130 years.

3. Be sure the students understand why English, Dutch, and French are the official languages of Guyana, Surinam, and French Guiana.

4. Choose a favorite sport of Venezuela such as soccer, (futbol), bull chasing, or water sports. Learn how it is played. Then explain it to your classmates. You may do any recreation listed in your LIFEPAC under Venezuela. Check with your teacher if the activity involves activity outside the classroom.

5. Make a picture of each of the flags of Venezuela, Guyana, Surinam, and French Guiana. Add them to your scrapbook of flags. If you prefer, you could make a wall display of your flags on poster card. Save this project to add the flags of other South American countries you will study in LIFEPAC 606.

6. If you wish, you may add wildlife and flowers of these countries to the notebook you have started.

# ANSWER KEYS

## SECTION 1

**1.1**   Teacher check
**1.2**   a.  northern
**1.3**   c.  equator
**1.4**   c.  Indians
**1.5**   c.  tall trees
**1.6**   b.  rubber
**1.7**   Teacher check
**1.8**   Any order:
    a.  central
    b.  humid
    c.  cool
    d.  coffee growing
    e.  east to west
**1.9**   a.  little rainfall
    b.  northeastern Brazil
    d.  short grasses
    e.  loyal citizen
    f.  drought
**1.10**  Examples:
    a.  seashore
    b.  abruptly
    c.  big
    d.  bearable
    e.  close
**1.11**  Teacher check
**1.12**  I.  Mineral Resources
    Any order:
    a. iron ore
    b. manganese
    c. gold
    d. diamonds
    e. bauxite
    II.  Farm Products
    Any order:
    a. coffee
    b. sugarcane
    c. cacao
    d. cotton
    e. rice
    f. corn
    g. potatoes
    h. wheat
    III. Animals
    Any order:
    a. hog
    b. sheep
    c. cattle

IV.  Rivers and Streams
    Any order:
    a. water power
    b. transportation
    c. home for fish
**1.13**  near the coast
**1.14**  Portuguese
**1.15**  slaves
**1.16**  c
**1.17**  a
**1.18**  d
**1.19**  b
**1.20**  f
**1.21**  a.  land
    b.  rich
    c.  poor
    d.  overseers
    e.  factory
    f.  modern
    g.  big businesses
    h.  plantations
    i.  industries
    j.  wages
    k.  middle class
**1.22**  d
**1.23**  g
**1.24**  e
**1.25**  h
**1.26**  c
**1.27**  a
**1.28**  b
**1.29**  false
**1.30**  false
**1.31**  true
**1.32**  true
**1.33**  true
**1.34**  false

**1.35**
a. regent
b. reduce
c. colonial
d. Portuguese
e. hat
f. Independence or death
g. September 7, 1822
h. Independence
i. constitution
j. constitutional
k. monarchy
l. government
m. four
n. abdicated
o. five
p. fifteen
q. 1841
r. fifty
s. slavery

**1.36** It resembles the United States Constitution
**1.37** He was not elected, but ruled like a king. He was a dictator.
**1.38** Kubitschek established Brasilia.
**1.39** Brazil has had a military democracy.
**1.40** Examples:
a. biggest
b. similar (to)
c. persons
d. nearest
e. businesses, trade
**1.41** e
**1.42** d
**1.43** b
**1.44** a
**1.45** c
**1.46** Example:
Carnival or Mardi Gras—days preceding Ash Wednesday or Lent. Ash Wednesday—first day of Lent. In some churches ashes are placed on the forehead of believers to remind them that they are "dust" and should love and obey God. Lent—forty days of fasting and penance before Easter. Carnival, then, is the last day of feasting before Easter.

**1.47** Sao Paulo
**1.48**
a. food
b. clothing
c. medicine
d. steel and machinery
e. cement
f. paper or paint, furniture, autos, tires
**1.49** "Order and Progress" is the national motto.
**1.50** The new law requires that every town must have an elementary school.
**1.51** Example:
This law will be difficult to carry out because of the cost of buildings and the increasing number of children.
**1.52** Any order:
a. air
b. roads
c. water
**1.53** Example:
a. By translating the Bible into their language
b. By making Gospel recordings in their language
c. By providing aviation service for natives and missionaries or by providing Gospel radio programs
**1.54** Example:
It is a requirement that all schools must make religious instruction available. Christian organizations in the United States have provided them with Bibles.
**1.55** Teacher check

# SELF TEST 1

| | | |
|---|---|---|
| **1.01** | c. | many cities |
| **1.02** | d. | equator |
| **1.03** | a. | steep mountains |
| **1.04** | a. | a synonym |
| **1.05** | b. | large woman |
| **1.06** | d. | hydroelectric plant |
| **1.07** | b. | tapir |
| **1.08** | c. | feijoada |
| **1.09** | b. | coffee |
| **1.010** | a. | Europe, mostly Portugal |
| **1.011** | b. | they were brought as slaves |
| **1.012** | d. | middle class |
| **1.013** | c. | captaincies |
| **1.014** | c. | Tiradentes |
| **1.015** | d. | Portugal |
| **1.016** | c | |
| **1.017** | l | |
| **1.018** | h | |
| **1.019** | f | |
| **1.020** | g | |
| **1.021** | m | |
| **1.022** | i | |
| **1.023** | o | |
| **1.024** | d | |
| **1.025** | e | |
| **1.026** | k | |
| **1.027** | b | |
| **1.028** | n | |

| | |
|---|---|
| **1.029** | a |
| **1.030** | Portugal |
| | Tiradentes |
| **1.031** | Rio de Janeiro or Brazil |
| | Dom Pedro I |
| | independence |
| **1.032** | fifty |
| | United States |
| | freeing or emancipation |
| **1.033** | São Paulo |
| **1.034** | Rio de Janeiro |
| **1.035** | capital |
| **1.036** | Carnival |
| **1.037** | soccer |
| **1.038** | São Paulo |
| **1.039** | Manaus |
| **1.040** | Examples: |
| | medical help, translating, teaching |
| **1.041** | true |
| **1.042** | true |
| **1.043** | false |
| **1.044** | false |
| **1.045** | false |
| **1.046** | true |
| **1.047** | false |
| **1.048** | true |

# SECTION 2

| | | |
|---|---|---|
| **2.1** | map check | |
| **2.2** | map check | |
| **2.3** | Cauca | |
| **2.4** | Magdalena | |
| **2.5** | from 3,000 to 7,000 feet | |
| **2.6** | fertile Valleys | |
| **2.7** | Caribbean Sea | |
| **2.8** | commercial freight | |
| **2.9** | Orinoco | |

**2.10** Animals
  a. iguanas
  b. armadillos
  c. monkeys
  d. deer
  e. capybara
  f. jaguar or puma
     wild hog
River and Sea
  g. piranhas
  h. crocodiles
  i. tropical fish
  j. salmon
  k. trout
  l. catfish
  m. marlin
  n. sailfish
  o. dolphin
  p. tuna
  q. lobster
  r. squid
  s. oyster
  t. haddock
  u. barracuda
  v. sea bass
Birds
  w. toucans
  x. heron
  y. hummingbirds
  z. exotic birds

**2.11** Teacher check

**2.12** Any order:
  a. emeralds
  b. platinum
  c. gold

**2.13** Either order:
  a. beef
  b. leather

**2.14** fish
**2.15** salt
**2.16** e. sculpture
**2.17** a. earth ridges
**2.18** c. miners

**2.19** b. conquistadors
**2.20** h. slaves
**2.21** d. official language
**2.22** f. 75%
**2.23** a. cooked in the shell
**2.24** b. ruanas
**2.25** c. makeshift dwellings
**2.26** b. coffee
**2.27** c. good homes
**2.28** a. Carib
**2.29** b. on seashores and mountains

**2.30**
  a. Indian Chief
  b. gold
  c. wife
  d. where

**2.31**
  a. much
  b. where
  c. easy

**2.32**
  a. treasure
  b. worth

**2.33** grow
**2.34** 1550

**2.35**
  a. Indians
  b. nothing
  c. patrons or landowners
  d. tribute

**2.36**
  a. Venezuela
  b. Ecuador
  c. Panama

**2.37**
  a. freedom
  b. Spain

**2.38** f
**2.39** d
**2.40** e
**2.41** b
**2.42** a

**2.43**
  a. Bolívar
  b. Liberator
  c. defeated
  d. Spanish
  e. Santander
  f. President
  g. Republic
  h. Santander
  i. Vice
  j. tyrant
  k. liberating
  l. Venezuela
  m. Ecuador
  n. banished
  o. 1830
  p. hero

**2.44** a. One wants a rich class.
b. The other wants to help the poor.
**2.45** a. Presidents were elected from alternate parties for a four-year term.
b. Government offices divided evenly between parties.
**2.46** map check
**2.47** Examples:
a. Gold Museum, Salt Cathedral, high altitude, 59° temperature all year, Capital of Colombia
b. Textiles, cool climate, orchids everywhere
c. Major seaport; city wall against pirates
d. At the mouth of Magdalena River
e. Banana shipping; Bolívar's death
f. Oil export; most important port
g. Oil export; southern point of Colombia's coast
h. Export zoo animals, hunters, extreme southeast corner
**2.48** Too few people have nearly all of the money. The poor far outnumber the rich.
**2.49** National Federation of Coffee Growers
**2.50** It gives loans for small farmers and businessmen.
**2.51** Teacher check

## SELF TEST 2

**2.01** b. exhibits gold treasures
**2.02** d. shortly after he was banished
**2.03** d. west
**2.04** d. a few people have most of the money
**2.05** a. fertile valleys
**2.06** b. Indians worked for no pay
**2.07** a. a group of citizens
**2.08** b. cotton or wool
**2.09** true
**2.010** false
**2.011** false
**2.012** false
**2.013** false
**2.014** true
**2.015** false
**2.016** false
**2.017** false
**2.018** true
**2.019** false
**2.020** false
**2.021** j
**2.022** l
**2.023** k
**2.024** c
**2.025** f
**2.026** e
**2.027** i
**2.028** b
**2.029** h
**2.030** m
**2.031** a
**2.032** g
**2.033** n
**2.034** d
**2.035** Either order:
a. He was a tyrant.
b. He was often away from the country.
**2.036** Either order:
a. Each party should serve alternate four-year terms.
b. All government offices were divided equally between members of the two parties.
**2.037** Spanish
**2.038** São Paulo
**2.039** Magdalena-Cauca
**2.040** coffee
**2.041** Panama Canal
**2.042** Portuguese
**2.043** pirate
**2.044** one who exercises absolute authority
**2.045** grassland
**2.046** a council or a council of citizens

# SECTION 3

**3.1** e

**3.2** j

**3.3** i

**3.4** f

**3.5** d

**3.6** a

**3.7** h

**3.8** b

**3.9** k

**3.10** c

**3.11** map check

**3.12** one thousand

**3.13** Orinoco

**3.14** a. 600
b. dredged

**3.15** hydroelectric

**3.16** Negro

**3.17** Teacher check

**3.18** a. mestizos
b. temple
c. village
d. stone
e. Timote
f. Quirquire
g. insects
h. Chake
i. arrows
j. fortified
k. Spanish
l. landowners
m. 75 per cent
n. individuals
o. wages

**3.19** Spain

**3.20** Little Venice

**3.21** pirates

**3.22** Earthly Paradise

**3.23** Caribbean Sea

**3.24** They could not understand and were not ready for democracy.

**3.25** He was called the Tyrant

**3.26** He stayed in power for 27 years.

**3.27** The citizens are pleased with their new government.

**3.28** a. Caracas; Examples:
1. capital of Venezuela
2. has statue of Bolívar in center of city
b. Maracaibo; Examples:
1. second largest
2. rich from oil in the lake
c. La Asuncion; Examples:
1. founded in 1824
2. once the center of the pearl industry

**3.29** Teacher check

**3.30** b

**3.31** d

**3.32** f

**3.33** a

**3.34** e

**3.35** Orinoco River

**3.36** airplane

**3.37** imported

**3.38** Robinson Crusoe

**3.39** cannibals

**3.40** inland

**3.41** a. 1970
b. British

**3.42** sugar

**3.43** bauxite

**3.44** read

**3.45** Dr. John Giglioli

**3.46** naturalists

**3.47** New Amsterdam
read and write
dikes, sea walls, sluice, gates
Dutch settlers
Hindustanis

**3.48** political

**3.49** less dangerous

**3.50** 1946

**3.51** 1946

**3.52** Cayenne

**3.53** Teacher check

# SELF TEST 3

| | | |
|---|---|---|
| **3.01** | b. | an airport |
| **3.02** | a. | 5% of the people |
| **3.03** | c. | petroleum |
| **3.04** | d. | 130 years |
| **3.05** | a. | growing |
| **3.06** | b. | ponchot |
| **3.07** | a. | Venice |
| **3.08** | d. | pearls |
| **3.09** | d. | Dutch |
| **3.010** | a. | Carib |
| **3.011** | u | |
| **3.012** | n | |
| **3.013** | d | |
| **3.014** | f | |
| **3.015** | i | |
| **3.016** | l | |
| **3.017** | b | |
| **3.018** | s | |
| **3.019** | e | |
| **3.020** | h | |
| **3.021** | p | |

| | | |
|---|---|---|
| **3.022** | a | |
| **3.023** | m | |
| **3.024** | c | |
| **3.025** | k | |
| **3.026** | t | |
| **3.027** | o | |
| **3.028** | g | |
| **3.029** | q | |
| **3.030** | j | |
| **3.031** | New York or New Amsterdam | |
| **3.032** | mixed | |
| **3.033** | a. | Indians |
| | b. | Bush Blacks |
| **3.034** | civilized | |
| **3.035** | lightning | |
| **3.036** | Orinoco | |
| **3.037** | Lake Maracaibo | |
| **3.038** | futbol | |
| **3.039** | Caracas | |
| **3.040** | bumble bee | |
| **3.041** | A rain forest has high trees that grow closely together. A jungle has low, thick grasses, trees, bushes, and vines. | |
| **3.042** | Lució Costa | |

# LIFEPAC TEST

| | | | | |
|---|---|---|---|---|
| I. | g | | 27. | Paramaribo |
| 2. | d | | 28. | Cayenne |
| 3. | i | | 29. | President |
| 4. | a | | 30. | offices |
| 5. | h | | 31. | 1830 |
| 6. | b | | 32. | Santander |
| 7. | l | | 33. | false |
| 8. | j | | 34. | true |
| 9. | c | | 35. | true |
| 10. | f | | 36. | false |
| 11. | m | | 37. | false |
| 12. | e | | 38. | true |
| 13. | a. water | | 39. | true |
| 14. | d. bauxite | | 40. | true |
| 15. | a. soil and ocean water | | 41. | false |
| 16. | d. a penal colony | | 42. | true |
| 17. | d. coffee | | 43. | d |
| 18. | b. Sugar Loaf Mountain | | 44. | f |
| 19. | b. bauxite | | 45. | a |
| 20. | a. in mountain cities and sea coasts | | 46. | b |
| 21. | b. gold | | 47. | c |
| 22. | a. battle of Carabobo | | 48. | pirate |
| 23. | Brasilia | | 49. | a wide plain |
| 24. | Bogota | | | |
| 25. | Caracas | | | |
| 26. | Georgetown | | | |

# ALTERNATE LIFEPAC TEST

1. true
2. false
3. true
4. true
5. false
6. false
7. true
8. true
9. false
10. true
11. Venezuela
12. Guyana
13. Brazil
14. Surinam
15. Colombia
16. French Guiana
17. petroleum or oil
18. prison or penal island (jail is acceptable)
19. democracy
20. pearls or pearl oysters
21. e
22. d
23. b
24. a
25. b. mountain of iron

26. d. alternate presidents every four years
27. d. a few people have most of the money
28. d. Dutch
29. c. a liberator and a tyrant
30. b. Chief of Gold
31. b. dentist
32. a. on the coastline
33. b. colonial period
34. b. Colombia
35. one who runs for office
36. a banana-like fruit
37. generating electricity by water power
38. a staple South American food from the root of the cassava plant. (A root used for food is acceptable.)
39. j
40. f
41. g
42. b
43. d
44. c
45. h
46. e
47. a
48. k

# HISTORY & GEOGRAPHY 605

## ALTERNATE LIFEPAC TEST

**NAME** _____

**DATE** _____

**SCORE** _____

80

100

**Answer true or false** (each answer, 1 point).

1. _____  Pelé played soccer for Brazil before playing in the United States.

2. _____  The major export of Surinam is orange juice.

3. _____  French Guiana has a space and missile center.

4. _____  King John ruled Portugal from Brazil.

5. _____  Colombia has one major ridge of mountains.

6. _____  The tapir is Brazil's smallest animal.

7. _____  In South America, Christmas comes in the summertime.

8. _____  The salt cathedral, near Bogotá, Colombia, is carved in a mountain of salt.

9. _____  The official language of Brazil is Spanish.

10. _____  The *ruana* is a favorite type of shawl worn in Colombia and other South American countries.

**Write the correct word on each line** (each answer, 3 points).

11. Caracas is the capital of _____ .

12. Georgetown is the capital of _____ .

13. Brasilia is the capital of _____ .

14. Paramaribo is the capital of _____ .

15. Bogotá is the capital of _____ .

16. Cayenne is the capital of _____ .

17. Venezuela's chief export and industry is _____ .

18. Devil's Island, off the coast of French Guiana, used to be a very bad _____ .

19. In Colombia, Santander was famous for planting seeds of _____ .

20. The waters around Venezuela's Margarita Island were once full of _____ .

**Match these items** (each answer, 2 points).

21. _____ Sugar Loaf Mountain

22. _____ Gold Museum

23. _____ spices

24. _____ Butana Snake Institute

a. Sao Paulo, Brazil

b. Cayenne, French Guiana

c. Caracas, Venezuela

d. Bogotá, Colombia

e. Rio de Janeiro, Brazil

**Write the correct letter and answer on each line** (each answer, 2 points).

25. "Cerro Bolívar" is a _____ .
    a. statue of Bolívar    b. mountain of iron    c. street in Caracas    d. food

26. The National Front in Colombia agreed that its two political parties would

    _____ .
    a. combine into one party            b. continue fighting
    c. form a third party                d. alternate presidents every four years

27. The sentence, "Wealth is not distributed evenly," means that _____ .
    a. wealth is for men only            b. children do not get allowances
    c. no dollar bills are made          d. a few people have most of the money

28. The Guianas learned to build dikes and sea walls from the _____ .
    a. Africans                          b. United States
    c. Chinese                           d. Dutch

29. Bolívar was _____ .
    a. a kind humanitarian               b. a lifetime resident of Colombia
    c. A liberator and a tyrant          d. very tall

30. *El Dorado* means _____ .
    a. land ho!                          b. Chief of Gold
    c. Gold Lake                         d. the great one

31. Tiradentes, Brazil freedom fighter, was a _____ .
    a. medical doctor    b. dentist        c. barber              d. veterinarian

**32.** Most people in Brazil live _____ .
   a. on the coastline        b. in the rain forests
   c. above ten thousand feet        d. on the grasslands

**33.** A time of growth for a country is the _____ .
   a. political period        b. colonial period
   c. conqueror's period        d. period of the buccaneer

**34.** The first airline in South America was established in _____ .
   a. Guyana        b. Colombia
   c. Brazil        d. Venezuela

**Write the correct definition on each line** (each answer, 3 points).

**35.** A candidate is _____ .

**36.** Plantain is _____ .

**37.** Hydroelectric means _____ .

**38.** Manioc is _____ .

**Match these items** (each answer, 2 points).

**39.** _____ stilt houses        a. size of a bumble bee

**40.** _____ bauxite        b. above ten thousand feet

**41.** _____ National Front        c. until 1966, owned by England

**42.** _____ grazing        d. bank that makes small loans

**43.** _____ Colombia's CAJA        e. Bolívar

**44.** _____ Guyana        f. aluminum

**45.** _____ 130 years of dictatorship        g. Colombia

**46.** _____ the Great Liberator        h. Venezuela

**47.** _____ Venezuela's hummingbirds        i. an orchid

**48.** _____ capybara        j. protect from animals and water

                                              k. large mouse-like animal

# HISTORY & GEOGRAPHY 606

Unit 6: Other South American Countries

# TEACHING NOTES

| MATERIALS NEEDED FOR LIFEPAC | |
|---|---|
| Required | Suggested |
| (None) | • encyclopedias<br>• maps - many different kinds of maps of South America showing populations, physical conditions, industries, wildlife, and so forth.<br>• (the reference materials can be either in book or online formats) |

## ADDITIONAL LEARNING ACTIVITIES

### Section 1: Ecuador, Peru, and Bolivia

1. Help direct students in their thinking as you go over maps with them. Help them to perceive how the physical aspects of a country will affect the people of that country. Be sure to point out the path of the Peru Current in the Pacific. Point out that Cuzco, the Inca capital, was in the high mountains of the Andes. Be sure the students know the location of Lake Titicaca, already mentioned in map studies.

2. Invite a missionary to speak to the class on work in South America. You may wish to question him about the training required to do missionary work. Perhaps he can tell the students how the decision was made to follow this calling.

3. If a missionary is not available, perhaps a Christian in your city has been to South America and can be invited to speak to the class.

4. Either keep the South American room display you made for LIFEPAC 605 or make a new one. Perhaps this time you could make a bulletin board display of these seven countries of South America.

5. With a classmate or classmates, try to make a musical instrument like those mentioned in your LIFEPAC. If several of you make different instruments, maybe you could play a musical piece together.

6. Make a poster display for your room of Inca artifacts as presented in various magazines and books.

7. Continue, if you wish, your scrapbook on the wildlife and wildflowers of South America you started for LIFEPAC 605. Begin a new one for this LIFEPAC if you like.

8. Continue with your display of flags by adding the flags of Ecuador, Peru, and Bolivia.

9. Make a mask like those mentioned in Section 1. You might have to do some research on the kind of masks men of the Indian countries make for festivals. Be sure you make it to fit you. If you do not want to wear it, perhaps you can hang it on the wall of your room at home.

10. *Charqui* of llama meat and jerky of beef was made this way in the early days: "Take long, thin strips of lean meat with the fat removed. Salt and pepper the strips, then hang them over a rope line or a tree limb, where they can get sun all day. Take inside at night or if it rains. Leave in sun for about a week. Meat strips should be dry but not hard. They will keep indefinitely if stored in a dry place."

Make some jerky for yourself by cutting lean meat without any fat into very thin strips.

Stretch the strips on baking racks that have been placed over cookie pans (to catch drippings). Salt and pepper the meat strips. Put the racks with meat and cookie pan in your oven at home and bake slowly all night (10 to 2 hours) at a temperature of 150 to 175 degrees. You might take your jerky to school and give your teacher plus some of your classmates a taste.

11. Measure the distance from your waistline to your knee. Then, on a large piece of butcher paper, an old sheet, or drape, mark a circle with a diameter twice as wide as the measurement you just determined. Be sure you have a perfect circle. Now cut the circle out. In the exact center cut a hole with the circumference the size of your waistline. Cut one straight line from the middle circle to the outside. Now put your circle on around your waist and fasten at the opening. You have a circular skirt similar to the ones the women of Bolivia wear. You may use it the way it is or decorate it.

12. Make a centerpiece for your table at home or at a church supper using as many of the vegetables mentioned in the reading on Food in your LIFEPAC as you can find. Most grocery stores carry nearly all of them year round. After you have finished, tell those sitting at the table that these are all vegetables native to South America.

## Section 2: Uruguay and Paraguay

1. It is important that students be guided in their studies of maps. Help them to understand the usefulness of seashores to the life of Uruguay, and the limited quality of life in a land-locked country like Paraguay.

2. Lead a discussion with the students. Let them imagine they are in charge of Paraguay's government. What methods would they use to build up the population of Paraguay? Be sure the students realize the population of this country is low because of repeated wars.

3. With a fellow student, make a poster picture of a South American *gaucho*. Dress him in traditional clothes and give him a *boleadora*.

4. *Yerba Maté* is sold in many health food stores in the United States. If your parents and teachers consent, you might purchase some. Bring it to class and show it to other students, explaining where the leaves come from and how they are used. Also tell what ways South Americans depend on this beverage. You might want another student to help you.

5. Make a travel poster advertising the resorts on Uruguay's coastline. You will have to learn some of the names of those resort cities to do this project.

6. Try to find out all you can about the spider-web lace made by the women of Paraguay. Perhaps you may be able to find someone who makes this kind of lace. If you can, perhaps you can bring a sample of it to class. If not, show your teacher pictures of the lace you have found.

7. Make pictures of the flags of Uruguay and Paraguay for your display.

8. Add to your scrapbook on the wildlife and flowers of South America.

## Section 3: Argentina and Chile

1. Point out the bleakness of Patagonia and Tierra del Fuego. Also mention the islands and waterways of Chile, showing the possibility of great change in case of earthquakes. Point out the closeness of the southern tip of Chile to the south Polar region. Explain the reason for the "southern lights."

2. Falcons and condors frequent the high Andes in Chile and the northern countries of South America. Someone in your city may train falcons or eagles. Ask him to talk to the class about his hobby. (Sometimes high schools havefalcon clubs.) If a speaker cannot be found, find an article on falconry (or condors and eagles). Show it to the students and let them ask questions about these majestic birds.

3. Make a model of a Spanish ship such as Magellan used. If it is not possible to make a model, make a picture of one or cut one out of a magazine. You will want to do this project with a classmate. Learn all you can about these boats; then explain it to the class.

4. Find a picture of the statue of Christ that stands between Argentina and Chile. Show this picture to classmates. Try to decide if the statue has helped relations between the two countries. You will have to do some research on this subject.

5. Add to your scrapbook on wildlife and wildflowers.

6. Make pictures of flags of Argentina and Chile for you display.

7. Choose Santiago, Chile, or Buenos Aires, Argentina. Find out all you can about the city you choose. Make lists of:

    a. the people who live there

    b. names of streets

    c. landmarks

    d. industries

8. Make an outline map of South America on a piece of cardboard. (The lid of a shoe box if fine.) Take clay to make mountains around the near-edge of the continent where they belong. Be sure to consult a physical map of South America for, as you know, some mountains are higher than others, some are further inland than others. Try to be as accurate as possible. Draw or paint in the major rivers such as the Amazon, the Paraguay, the Uruguay, the Pilcomayo, the Parana, and the Plata Estuary. You may also want to color in the jungle areas, rain forests, the Chaco, and the bleak southlands. Put some small buckshot or rice or cereal in the middle of your map to represent people. Now roll these around gently. How far to the outside can your people get over the natural physical barriers? Not very far. Put some "people" on the coastline outside the mountains. How far can they get inland over the mountains? Make the islands of lower Chile out of small bits of clay. Shake your map slightly and the clay will move much in the same manner the earth moves during an earthquake.

# ANSWER KEYS

## SECTION 1

**1.1** two
**1.2** steaming
**1.3** earthquakes
**1.4** 400
**1.5** three
**1.6** altiplano
**1.7** large
**1.8** eastern
**1.9** western
**1.10** western
**1.11** western
**1.12** eastern
**1.13** eastern
**1.14** western
**1.15** western
**1.16** <u>Oriente</u>
    puma
    snakes
    tapirs
    <u>Andes</u>
    falcons
    condors
    llama
    <u>Seacoast</u>
    tuna
    shrimp
    crayfish
    lobster
    <u>Galapagos</u>
    wild horses
    albatrosses
    iguana
    wild dogs
    pelicans
    wild cattle
    tortoises
    finches
**1.17** a. scarce
    b. full
    c. giant
    d. exist, live
    e. most
    f. fine
    g. heavy
    h. thick
    i. docile
**1.18** false
**1.19** true
**1.20** true

**1.21** true
**1.22** false
**1.23** false
**1.24** false
**1.25** false
**1.26** Teacher check
**1.27** Teacher check
**1.28** Teacher check
**1.29** Teacher check
**1.30** true
**1.31** true
**1.32** false
**1.33** false
**1.34** false
**1.35** n
**1.36** k
**1.37** f
**1.38** m
**1.39** o
**1.40** d
**1.41** g
**1.42** c
**1.43** h
**1.44** a
**1.45** l
**1.46** i
**1.47** e
**1.48** b
**1.49** festivals
**1.50** Spanish
**1.51** dialects
**1.52** Any one:
    a. potatoes
    b. pumpkins
    c. squash
    d. corn
    e. peanuts
**1.53** heavy or warm
**1.54** huts or complexes
**1.55** written
**1.56** sun god
**1.57** 1450
**1.58** Cuzco
**1.59** a. gold
    b. silver
**1.60** irrigation
**1.61** true
**1.62** false
**1.63** false

**1.64** true

**1.65** false

**1.66** conquer<u>or</u>, conquer, verb, noun

**1.67** histor<u>ian</u>, history, noun, noun

**1.68** center<u>ed</u>, center, verb or noun, verb past tense

**1.69** irrig<u>ation</u>, irrigate, verb noun

**1.70** govern<u>ment</u>, govern, verb, noun

**1.71** expedi<u>tion</u>, expedite, verb noun

**1.72** remind<u>ers</u>, remind, verb, noun

**1.73** colon<u>ial</u>, colony, noun, adjective

**1.74** organiz<u>ed</u>, organize, verb, verb past tense

**1.75** fertil<u>izer</u>, fertile, adjective, noun

**1.76** free<u>dom</u>, free, verb or adjective, noun

**1.77** dictat<u>or</u>, dictate, verb, noun

**1.78** defeat<u>ed</u>, defeat, verb or noun, verb past tense

**1.79** nation<u>al</u>, nation, noun, adjective

**1.80** obvious<u>ly</u>, obvious, adjective, adverb

**1.81** liberat<u>ors</u>, liberate, verb, noun

**1.82** unhapp<u>ily</u>, unhappy, adjective, adverb

**1.83** libera<u>tion</u>, liberate, verb, noun

**1.84** Colombia is north of Ecuador.

**1.85** The Galápagos Islands belong to Ecuador.

**1.86** They are 600 miles to the west.

**1.87** Quito is the capital city.

**1.88** Guayaquil is the chief port.

**1.89** It is at the mouth of the Guayas River.

**1.90** Ecuador's chief resource and industry is bananas.

**1.91** c

**1.92** b

**1.93** h

**1.94** f

**1.95** a

**1.96** g

**1.97** e

**1.98** seacoast

**1.99** west

**1.100** Brazil

**1.101** Sucre

**1.102** tin

**1.103** Teacher check

**1.104** Teacher check

**1.105** k

**1.106** l

**1.107** d

**1.108** c

**1.109** h

**1.110** b

**1.111** f

**1.112** g

**1.113** i

**1.114** j

**1.115** a

# SELF TEST 1

| | | | | |
|---|---|---|---|---|
| **1.01** | false | | **1.029** | b |
| **1.02** | false | | **1.030** | a |
| **1.03** | false | | **1.031** | c |
| **1.04** | true | | **1.032** | b |
| **1.05** | false | | **1.033** | a |
| **1.06** | true | | **1.034** | d |
| **1.07** | true | | **1.035** | c |
| **1.08** | true | | **1.036** | b |
| **1.09** | false | | **1.037** | d |
| **1.010** | false | | **1.038** | e |
| **1.011** | true | | **1.039** | f |
| **1.012** | false | | **1.040** | a |
| **1.013** | true | | **1.041** | b |
| **1.014** | false | | **1.042** | c |
| **1.015** | true | | **1.043** | sun god |
| **1.016** | false | | **1.044** | Inca |
| **1.017** | true | | **1.045** | Spain |
| **1.018** | false | | **1.046** | dictator or despots |
| **1.019** | false | | **1.047** | bananas |
| **1.020** | true | | **1.048** | wheel |
| **1.021** | c | | **1.049** | stones (blocks) |
| **1.022** | a | | **1.050** | gold (silver or both) |
| **1.023** | d | | **1.051** | San Martin |
| **1.024** | c | | **1.052** | vanadium |
| **1.025** | a | | **1.053** | Jose de Sucre |
| **1.026** | a | | **1.054** | tin |
| **1.027** | a | | | |
| **1.028** | a | | | |

# SECTION 2

| | |
|---|---|
| 2.1 | cold |
| 2.2 | 120 |
| 2.3 | a. Atlantic |
| | b. Brazil |
| | c. Argentina |
| 2.4 | Plata |
| 2.5 | Negro River |
| 2.6 | western |
| 2.7 | Teacher check |
| 2.8 | l |
| 2.9 | j |
| 2.10 | d |
| 2.11 | h |
| 2.12 | f |
| 2.13 | c |
| 2.14 | e |
| 2.15 | m |
| 2.16 | b |
| 2.17 | g |
| 2.18 | k |
| 2.19 | a |
| 2.20 | false |
| 2.21 | true |
| 2.22 | true |
| 2.23 | false |
| 2.24 | true |
| 2.25 | false |
| 2.26 | true |
| 2.27 | false |
| 2.28 | true |
| 2.29 | false |
| 2.30 | Teacher check |

**2.31-2.33** Examples; Any order:

2.31 Montevideo - capital, chief city, has three parts

2.32 Colonia - by the Plata, historical landmarks

2.33 Salto - by Uruguay River, gaucho town, tourists

**2.34-2.41** Examples:

2.34 chief resource

2.35 source of income

2.36 Lobos Island, source of income

2.37 Russian, British, and Scandinavian fishermen

2.38 almost all the land is used for this

2.39 want to get away from the cold

2.40 new source of income

2.41 third largest industry

2.42 Teacher check

2.43 true

2.44 false

2.45 true

2.46 false

2.47 false

2.48 true

2.49 true

2.50 false

2.51 true

2.52 false

2.53 Either order:
a. Carlos Lopez
b. Alfredo Stroessner

2.54 Either order:
a. Jose de Francia
b. Francisco Lopez

2.55 Teacher check

2.56 Teacher check

**2.57-2.60** Examples:

2.57 Ascunción - capital, largest, seven hills, Hotel Guarani, gardens, names of streets

2.58 Encarnación - old Jesuit village, tornado destroyed, new city

2.59 Primavera - "springtime", Hutterite, handmade items

2.60 Filadelfia - Mennonite, farmers, co-op stores

2.61 Teacher check

# SELF TEST 2

| | |
|---|---|
| **2.01** | false |
| **2.02** | true |
| **2.03** | false |
| **2.04** | false |
| **2.05** | true |
| **2.06** | true |
| **2.07** | true |
| **2.08** | false |
| **2.09** | false |
| **2.010** | true |
| **2.011** | true |
| **2.012** | false |
| **2.013** | true |
| **2.014** | false |
| **2.015** | true |
| **2.016** | true |
| **2.017** | true |
| **2.018** | true |
| **2.019** | true |
| **2.020** | true |
| **2.021** | m |
| **2.022** | n |
| **2.023** | j |
| **2.024** | c |
| **2.025** | e |
| **2.026** | g |
| **2.027** | b |
| **2.028** | a |
| **2.029** | f |
| **2.030** | o |
| **2.031** | i |
| **2.032** | p |
| **2.033** | d |
| **2.034** | q |
| **2.035** | h |
| **2.036** | k |
| **2.037** | Montevideo |
| **2.038** | Filadelfia |
| **2.039** | Ascunción |
| **2.040** | Salto |
| **2.041** | Uruguay |
| **2.042** | the Yerba tree, a tree |
| **2.043** | South America or Peru or Bolivia |
| **2.044** | high plains or high plateaus |
| **2.045** | blocks of stone |
| **2.046** | Bolivia |
| **2.047** | livestock or sheep and cattle |
| **2.048** | farm products or vegetables and fruit |
| **2.049** | British or English |
| **2.050** | Yerbe mate |
| **2.051** | Paraná |
| **2.052** | Rutherford B. Hayes |

# SECTION 3

**3.1** East
- k. Atlantic Ocean
- b. Mesopotamia

West
- g. Andes

North
- i. Gran Chaco
- b. Mesopotamia
- a. Paraná River
- f. Uruguay River

Central
- d. Pampas
- j. Colorado River

South
- c. Patagonia
- e. Strait of Magellan
- h. Tierra del Fuego

**3.2** Teacher check

**3.3** false

**3.4** true

**3.5** true

**3.6** true

**3.7** false

**3.8** false

**3.9** true

**3.10** The viceroy no longer had power because the King of Spain lost power to Napoleon.

**3.11** He disguised himself as a peasant.

**3.12** They did not know exactly why he was doing all the things he did.

**3.13** Juan Perón became president of Argentina two times.

**3.14** Perón's wife Eva was more popular than her husband.

**3.15** She helped the poor.

**3.16** She had been elected co-president or vice president.

**3.17** In Argentina it means the President is elected from the military ranks.

**3.18** Teacher check

**3.19** e

**3.20** c

**3.21** b

**3.22** g

**3.23** h

**3.24** d

**3.25** a

**3.26** Teacher check

**3.27** false

**3.28** true

**3.29** false

**3.30** false

**3.31** true
**3.32** true
**3.33** true
**3.34** false
**3.35** narrow
**3.36** north
**3.37** appear
**3.38** quickly
**3.39** leave
**3.40** light
**3.41** few
**3.42** urban or city
**3.43** summer
**3.44** higher
**3.45** comes
**3.46** e
**3.47** h
**3.48** i
**3.49** a
**3.50** g
**3.51** b
**3.52** d
**3.53** f
**3.54** Pizzaro and Almagro
**3.55** pirates
**3.56** regular postal service
**3.57** San Martin
**3.58** Bernardo O'Higgins
**3.59** sewers in Santiago
**3.60** War of the Pacific
**3.61** Allende
**3.62** Frei
**3.63** Chile buys back copper mines
**3.64** military government
**3.65** copper
**3.66** Either order:
    a. United States
    b. Great Britain
**3.67** Any order:
    a. steel or copper processing
    b. glassmaking
    c. porcelain
    d. paper
    e. flour or textiles
**3.68** Teacher check
**3.69** Teacher check
**3.70** Teacher check
**3.71** Teacher check

# SELF TEST 3

**3.01** false
**3.02** true
**3.03** true
**3.04** true
**3.05** true
**3.06** true
**3.07** true
**3.08** true
**3.09** true
**3.010** true
**3.011** false
**3.012** true
**3.013** false
**3.014** true
**3.015** true
**3.016** false
**3.017** true
**3.018** true
**3.019** false
**3.020** false
**3.021** o
**3.022** p
**3.023** m
**3.024** k
**3.025** c
**3.026** e
**3.027** f
**3.028** d
**3.029** h
**3.030** i
**3.031** j
**3.032** g
**3.033** n
**3.034** l
**3.035** a
**3.036** a
**3.037** d
**3.038** d
**3.039** c
**3.040** a
**3.041** d
**3.042** b
**3.043** Andes Mountains
**3.044** Patagonia
**3.045** Tierra del Fuego
**3.046** Cattle, beets, grains
**3.047** Paraná
**3.048** California
**3.049** Ecuador
**3.050** navigable
**3.051** bananas
**3.052** Cordoba

**3.053**  Patagonia, Tierra del Fuego
**3.054**  200 miles

# LIFEPAC TEST

| | |
|---|---|
| I. | true |
| 2. | false |
| 3. | true |
| 4. | true |
| 5. | false |
| 6. | false |
| 7. | true |
| 8. | a |
| 9. | c |
| 10. | d |
| 11. | d |
| 12. | c |
| 13. | b |
| 14. | b |
| 15. | c |
| 16. | c |
| 17. | c |
| 18. | a |
| 19. | a |

20-25 Examples:
20. Women make straw hats in Cuenca.
21. A large and old colony of Mennonites migrated to Filadelfia.
22. Salto is in gaucho country.
23. Primavera is the Hutterite community.
24. Cuzco was the capital of the Inca Empire.
25. The "Casa Historica" is a museum in Tucamán.
26. wars
27. Magellan
28. Lake Titicaca
29. meat
30. earthquakes
31. O'Higgins
32. gaucho
33. altiplanos
34-40. Any order for each country with its capital:
34.  a.  Chile
     b.  Santiago
35.  a.  Argentina
     b.  Buenos Aires
36.  a.  Paraguay
     b.  Asunción
37.  a.  Uruguay
     b.  Montevideo
38.  a.  Bolivia
     b.  La Paz and Sucre
39.  a   Peru
     b.  Lima
40.  a.  Ecuador
     b.  Quito

## ALTERNATE LIFEPAC TEST

| | | | | |
|---|---|---|---|---|
| 1. | i | 27. | false | |
| 2. | c | 28. | false | |
| 3. | k | 29. | true | |
| 4. | d | 30. | true | |
| 5. | f | 31. | true | |
| 6. | g | 32. | c. | vicuña |
| 7. | e | 33. | a. | Peru current |
| 8. | b | 34. | b. | Pizzaro |
| 9. | a | 35. | c. | the south |
| 10. | l | 36. | b | cotton |
| 11. | j | 37. | c. | an adjective |
| 12. | tin | 38. | c. | family pets |
| 13. | herb tea, tea, or drink | 39. | a. | four or five days |
| 14. | Ecuador | 40. | c. | Spanish |
| 15. | Chile | 41. | a. | derby hats |
| 16. | Pizzaro | 42. | bananas | |
| 17. | camel | 43. | Inca ruins | |
| 18. | bolo or boleadora | 44. | circular skirts | |
| 19. | Andes mountains | 45. | gauchos | |
| 20. | Titicaca | 46. | few people | |
| 21. | Argentina | 47. | smocks to school | |
| 22. | true | 48. | earthquakes | |
| 23. | true | 49. | true | |
| 24. | false | 50. | false | |
| 25. | false | 51. | false | |
| 26. | false | 52. | true | |

# HISTORY & GEOGRAPHY 606

## ALTERNATE LIFEPAC TEST

**NAME** _____

**DATE** _____

**SCORE** _____

80
—
100

**Match these items** (answers may be used more than once, each answer, 2 points).

1. _____ the Inca capital

2. _____ Ecuador's capital

3. _____ Paraguay's capital

4. _____ Argentine's capital

5. _____ Chile's capital

6. _____ Uruguay's capital

7. _____ Bolivia's capital in fact

8. _____ Bolivia's legal capital

9. _____ Mennonite city

10. _____ named after two Indians

11. _____ Peru's capital

a. Filadelfia

b. Sucre

c. Quito

d. Buenos Aires

e. La Paz

f. Santiago

g. Montevido

h. Tucamán

i. Cuzco

j. Lima

k. Ascunción

l. Guayaquil

**Write the correct answer on each line** (each answer, 3 points).

12. Cerro Rico and other mountains in Bolivia now are mined for _____ .

13. *Yerba Mate* is a _____ .

14. The Galapagos Islands are owned by _____ .

15. A country in South America which is only two hundred miles wide at its widest point is

_____ .

16. The name of the man whose expeditions conquered the Incas was _____ .

17. The llama family is cousin to the _____ .

18. The gaucho chief hunting tool is the _____ .

19. Chile is divided from Argentina by the _____ .

20. The highest navigable lake in the world is Lake _____ .

21. "Student Day" is celebrated in _____ .

**Answer true or false** (each answer, 1 point).

22. _____ Potatoes originated in Peru and Bolivia.

23. _____ Uruguay encourages much social welfare.

24. _____ Chile's earthquakes usually are very mild.

25. _____ Paraguay is overpopulated.

26. _____ Colorado Indians are called "the brown ones."

27. _____ Jungle Indians often shop in the big cities.

28. _____ An antonym is a word with the same meaning as another word.

29. _____ *Altiplanos* are high plateaus between the peaks of the *cordilleras*.

30. _____ *Leisure* means *free time from regular work*.

31. _____ The bleak region in South America named after "big feet" is Patagonia.

**Write the correct letter and answer on each line** (each answer, 2 points).

32. The South American animal with the finest wool is the _____ .
    a. sheep          b. lamb          c. vicuna          d. llama

33. The current that makes a complete circle in the Pacific, coming close to Peru's coast is the

_____ .
    a. Peru Current                    b. Westwind Current
    c. Galapagos Current               d. Ecuador Current

34. Machu Picchu, an Inca city in the plateaus of Peru, was never found by _____ .
    a. S. Cabot                        b. Pizzaro
    c. a United States senator         d. San Martin

35. San Martin was the South American liberator who worked from _____ .
    a. the jungles        b. the north        c. the south        d. Spain

36. On the desert coast of Peru is grown _____ .
    a. rubber        b. cotton        c. coffee        d. kapok

37. Adding -al to the noun nation changes the word to _____ .
    a. an adverb        b. a subject        c. an adjective        d. a preposition

38. Llamas and alpacas often become _____ .
    a. lame        b. unfriendly        c. family pets        d. useless

39. Uruguay has a work week of _____ .
    a. four or five days     b. forty-eight hours     c. seven days        d. ten hours

40. The official language of all countries studied in this LIFEPAC is _____ .
    a. Portuguese        b. English        c. Spanish        d. French

41. Bolivian women wear _____ .
    a. derby hats        b. bonnets        c. fedoras        d. beanies

**Write the word or phrase beside the country it is most associated with** (each answer, 2 points).

42. Ecuador _____        Inca ruins

43. Peru _____        smocks to school

44. Bolivia _____        few people

45. Uruguay_____        bananas

46. Paraguay_____        circular skirts

47. Argentina _____        earthquakes

48. Chile _____        gauchos

**Write true or false** (each answer, 1 point).

49. _____ Sucre fought more battles to free Ecuador and Bolivia than Bolívar did.

50. _____ San Martin and Bolívar died happy men.

51. _____ Magellan passed Ecuador on his voyage to the Orient.

52. _____ Auca Indians killed five missionaries.

# HISTORY & GEOGRAPHY 607

Unit 7: Africa

# TEACHING NOTES

| MATERIALS NEEDED FOR LIFEPAC | |
|---|---|
| Required | Suggested |
| (None) | • globe<br>• large map of Africa (the most recent available)<br>• (the reference materials can be either in book or online formats) |

## ADDITIONAL LEARNING ACTIVITIES

### Introduction

1. Research the Berlin Conference at the library or online. Re-enact the Conference and then discuss why the Europeans thought they should do this.

2. Collect news articles on Africa during the time you are studying this LIFEPAC. Discuss the articles at the end of the time.

3. Cut out a piece of cardboard in the shape of Africa. Using clay, create a topographical map of the continent. Find a creative way to show deserts, rain forests, the Sahel, and savanna on the map.

### Section 1: Northern Africa

1. Discuss these questions with your class.

    a. What change in climate made the Sahara Desert? (lack of rain)

    b. What could make the desert bloom again? (water by irrigation)

    c. Why did the people become nomads?

    d. Why were loose cotton clothes worn?

    e. Why did people travel in long caravans? (for safety and tribal unity)

    f. How did this strong tribal unity affect national unity in later years?

    g. Today, why would most northern African countries favor the Arabs? (many people are Arabs with Arab religion and customs)

    h. At one time Timbuktu (Tombouctou) was an important city in Mali. What invention changed its "end of road" status? (airplane)

    i. Why did a great civilization start in Egypt rather than in Niger or Chad?

2. Cooperate with the teacher to take a trip to a museum to study African artifacts. Take notes about the objects you find there.

3. On a poster board or a large sheet of wrapping paper, draw a large outline map of Africa. Cut out pictures, or draw them, of animals, birds, homes, people, children playing, trees, and so forth for the northern section of Africa. Paste them on your display. Be sure to save room for the other two sections of Africa.

4. Make a booklet about the camel. Draw or cut out pictures of camels. Write about its habits and value.

5. On a large piece of construction paper, start a collage of animals found in Africa. Paste the pictures close together, but keep the collage balanced. The pictures may be drawn or cut from old magazines. Know where each animal's habitat is and something about it.

6. If flags interest you, start now a display of the flags of North African countries. Either draw them yourself, cut out the pictures, or print online images. Under each flag tell what the colors and objects stand for. You may make a scrapbook, if you prefer, but plan on having many flags by the time you are through. Save room for the flags of Central and Southern Africa also.

7. Research and report to the class on the Empires of Ghana, Mali, or Songhai.

## Section 2: Central Africa

1. Discuss these questions with your class.

   a. Why did the white men stay out of equatorial Africa so long? (areas impenetrable, health hazards, little knowledge of jungle areas)

   b. How did missionaries help to open up this continent? (explored it)

   c. Why would the coastal plains be best suited to agriculture?

   d. Why are European influences still seen in Africa?

   e. Why was agriculture not stressed by European rulers? (precious minerals and ivory meant wealth. Food was imported.)

   f. Most countries have become independent since World War II. Why have they not done as well as before? (Rulers were often expelled and natives did not have the "know-how.")

2. Make a corner of your room to look like Africa in the Tropical Zone. Cut out vegetation from cardboard boxes and paint them. Make native hut villages out of mud or straw or whatever you have on hand. You will have to do some research to make this village authentic. Give your village a name. String a wire or clothesline across the entrance to it with letters spelling out the name.

3. Continue your display of Africa, started in Section 1. Add pictures of animals, birds, people, children, trees, and so forth from Central Africa.

4. Play a game. Describe an animal. Ask your friends to guess it. If they cannot, keep giving clues. The guesser is *it* next time.

5. Read a book, a section of a magazine, or online articles about a country in Central Africa. Write a report or give an oral resumé of what you read.

6. Add to your collage of animals of Africa. This time paste on animals and birds of Central Africa.

7. If you are making a display or scrapbook of flags, add the ones from the countries of Central Africa. This project is large but very rewarding if you do it well. Be sure to tell near the flag the meaning of the colors and objects on it.

8. Research the history of the ivory trade and how it has affected the African elephants. Write a report or give an oral report to the class.

9. Each student should research a different tribe in a single country in Africa. Discuss how the groups are different and the problems they would have working together.

10. Read a book on the slave trade. Write a story of one person being captured, sold to European slave traders, and taken to a colony in the Americas.

## Section 3: Southern Africa

1. Discuss these questions with your class.

   a. Why would we in the United States feel more at home if we visited South Africa rather than Central or Northern Africa? (climate, land surface, cities, activities, and European influence is much like ours.)

   b. Why is the country of South Africa so rich? What are its resources?

   c. If you wanted to visit Africa during the coolest season, when would you go?

   d. Why is Christmas so warm in Africa?

   e. If you were to go on a safari, why would you not be allowed to take a rifle or knife? (Animals cannot be killed.)

   f. What kind of safari would you go on then? (photographic)

   g. Can you guess why plastic coverings are important in Africa? (keep out insects, sand, and rain.)

2. Research the life of a person near your age in Africa. Compare his life with yours. When you have compiled all your information, write a skit about the differences between you, supposing perhaps one of you is visiting the other in the land of your birth. Give the skit before the classroom.

3. Pretend that each member of the class is a member of a tribe or race of Africa. One can be a nomad, another a miner, another a Bantu, and so forth. Dress up, if you wish, to play the part. Explain to other students what you are doing.

4. Complete your display started in Section 1. Add to it animals, birds, people, children, and so forth, of Southern Africa. When you have finished, explain your project to the rest of the classroom.

5. Choose one of the subjects:

   a. the early Christians of North Africa

   b. the python and other snakes of Africa

   c. the Nile River

   d. the crocodile

   e. the Congo River

   f. Dr. David Livingstone

   Do research on the subject you have chosen. When you get all your facts together, pretend you are a radio or television announcer. Explain your subject, "Ladies and gentlemen, I present to you the _____ of Africa. Did you know _____ ?" If you cannot do this project in the classroom, do it for your family at home.

6. Complete your collage with South African animals. When you have them all pasted on, mount your collage on a larger piece of paper and hang it either in your classroom or in your room at home.

7. Add to your flag display or scrapbook the flags of the countries of Southern Africa as listed in your LIFEPAC. Do not forget to mention the reason for the colors and objects on these flags. You will want to keep this display for a long time and show it to friends. You may find it useful in years to come.

8. Make a list of people or conditions in Africa that you would like to pray for. Show the list to your teacher. Together, discuss the fact that often prayer is the only way we can help a poor situation. Prayer often helps *more* than any other thing.

# ANSWER KEYS

## SECTION 1

**1.1** Dictators were able to stay in power with help from the Super Powers.

**1.2** Second.

**1.3** Slaves.

**1.4** Mediterranean Sea, Suez Canal, Red Sea, Indian Ocean, and Atlantic Ocean.

**1.5** Portuguese.

**1.6** European nations divided up Africa among themselves.

**1.7** Africa is in both Hemispheres because the Equator crosses through the center of it.

**1.8** In the 1960s.

**1.9** Tribalism. Each person is loyal to their tribe not the nation the Europeans created. (Exact words may vary).

**1.10** Disease and difficulty raising food.

**1.11** Debt owed to other nations that often can not be repaid.

**1.12** Gold and salt

**1.13** The Sahara Desert.

**1.14** Islam.

**1.15** By camel.

**1.16** An area of semi-desert along the southern edge of the Sahara.

**1.17** Ghana, Mali, and Songhai.

**1.18** Cape Verde

**1.19** Left.

**1.20** Morocco

**1.21** Constitutional Monarchy.

**1.22** France.

**1.23** It has valuable phosphate deposits.

**1.24** The white, European settlers.

**1.25** Teacher check

**1.26** South Sudan

**1.27** The Suez Canal allowed them to reach their territories in the Indian Ocean quickly.

**1.28** Islam.

**1.29** Darfur

**1.30** South to north.

**1.31** Made peace with Israel.

**1.32** Oil.

**1.33** Tunisia.

**1.34** Egypt, Republic of Sudan

**1.35** Republic of South Sudan, July 9, 2011

**1.36** Libya.

**1.37** Language, race, religion, amount of education and industry.

**1.38** Mali.

**1.39** The Niger River.

# SELF TEST 1

| | | | |
|---|---|---|---|
| **1.01** | South Sudan | **1.024** | i |
| **1.02** | Tunisia | **1.025** | e |
| **1.03** | Egypt | **1.026** | g |
| **1.04** | Morocco | **1.027** | h |
| **1.05** | Algeria | **1.028** | c |
| **1.06** | Libya | **1.029** | false |
| **1.07** | The Berlin Conference | **1.030** | false |
| **1.08** | An area of semi-desert on the southern edge of the Sahara Desert | **1.031** | true |
| | | **1.032** | true |
| **1.09** | Tribalism | **1.033** | true |
| **1.010** | Gold and salt | **1.034** | true |
| **1.011** | Islam (Muslim) | **1.035** | false |
| **1.012** | Cape Verde | **1.036** | true |
| **1.013** | Nothing, they are different words for the same thing. | **1.037** | true |
| | | **1.038** | false |
| **1.014** | The Mediterranean Sea | | |
| **1.015** | The Portuguese | | |
| **1.016** | Cold War | | |
| **1.017** | Desert | | |
| **1.018** | South to north | | |
| **1.019** | f | | |
| **1.020** | d | | |
| **1.021** | b | | |
| **1.022** | a | | |
| **1.023** | j | | |

**1.039** The stronger African ethnic groups captured their weaker neighbors and sold them to the Europeans.
(Do not need exact words).

**1.040** The Africans were not treated fairly by Europeans who sold them as slaves, took their land, and often only gave them their independence after a war was fought.
(Student may express their own ideas).

# SECTION 2

| | |
|---|---|
| **2.1** | Trade between the interior of Africa and the Middle East and India |
| **2.2** | The Great Rift Valley or The Rift system |
| **2.3** | Benin, Dahomey, Oyo |
| **2.4** | The Congo River Basin |
| **2.5** | Deforestation occurs when timber is overharvested or cleared for farmland. |
| **2.6** | Peanuts |
| **2.7** | Senegal |
| **2.8** | Blood diamonds were sold to support rebel fighters. |
| **2.9** | Guinea |
| **2.10** | Liberia |
| **2.11** | Freed American slaves |
| **2.12** | Culture, religion, and location. |
| **2.13** | Coffee, cocoa, palm products, peanuts, cotton, soy beans |
| **2.14** | political turmoil and civil war |
| **2.15** | Nigeria |
| **2.16** | The different religious groups control their own regions of the country |
| **2.17** | A democracy has been established. |
| **2.18** | Ibo, Hausa, Yoruba |
| **2.19** | Near the coast |
| **2.20** | Oil and trees |
| **2.21** | Cruelty against everyone for little or no reason by the government. |
| **2.22** | Mt. Cameroon |
| **2.23** | Roman Catholicism Because it is a former Spanish colony. |
| **2.24** | On the river, in boats, because the plant life in the jungle is too thick to walk through. |
| **2.25** | Central African Republic |
| **2.26** | Mt. Kilimanjaro in Tanzania |
| **2.27** | Lake Victoria |
| **2.28** | The Congo River Basin |
| **2.29** | Zanzibar |

| | |
|---|---|
| **2.30** | Genocide is the planned mass killing of a group of people based on their ethnic background. |
| **2.31** | Bad government, mismanagement and corruption |
| **2.32** | He has stolen a huge amount of money from Zaire |
| **2.33** | Tribal warfare |
| **2.34** | Lake Tanganyika |
| **2.35** | Copper |
| **2.36** | Anarchy and civil war |
| **2.37** | The ethnic conflicts between the Hutus and Tutsi people came from the years of Belgian control when the Tutsi people were favored. |
| **2.38** | A high number of people can read by African standards and they have a non-European national language— KiSwahili |
| **2.39** | Ethiopia |
| **2.40** | Clan warfare |
| **2.41** | The native people were trying to end rule by the Europeans settlers |
| **2.42** | It is at the mouth of the Red Sea and from there ships going to the Suez Canal could easily be attacked. |
| **2.43** | Poaching |
| **2.44** | Aksum |
| **2.45** | Tourism because of the many wild animals in the country. People come to photograph them. |
| **2.46** | War between the government and Eritrea |
| **2.47** | In the A.D. 300s |
| **2.48** | Semites and Cushites |
| **2.49** | outside Nairobi, Kenya in the Mathare Valley |
| **2.50** | Somalia |

## SELF TEST 2

| | |
|---|---|
| 2.01 | c |
| 2.02 | i |
| 2.03 | f |
| 2.04 | d |
| 2.05 | j |
| 2.06 | a |
| 2.07 | h |
| 2.08 | g |
| 2.09 | b |
| 2.010 | e |
| 2.011 | Congo River Basin |
| 2.012 | City-states |
| 2.013 | Photo safari |
| 2.014 | Mathare Valley |
| 2.015 | Tribal warfare |
| 2.016 | The Great Rift Valley |
| 2.017 | Tropical rain forest |
| 2.018 | Mass terror |
| 2.019 | One party government |
| 2.020 | multi-party governement |
| 2.021 | Djibouti |
| 2.022 | Liberia |
| 2.023 | Somalia |
| 2.024 | Nigeria |
| 2.025 | Uganda |
| 2.026 | Kenya |
| 2.027 | Rwanda |
| 2.028 | Ethiopia |
| 2.029 | Democratic Republic of the Congo |
| 2.030 | Tanzania |
| 2.031 | Government (bad, corrupt, unstable, etc.) |
| 2.032 | Islam, Christianity, and Traditional religions |
| 2.033 | Millet, corn (maize), cassava, bananas, or yams |
| 2.034 | Coffee, cocoa, tea, peanuts, cotton, palm products, rice, ginger, cloves, or tobacco |
| 2.035 | Biafra |
| 2.036 | War |
| 2.037 | It sits high in the mountains and is, therefore, hard to attack |
| 2.038 | African kingdoms on the west coast when the Portuguese arrived. |
| 2.039 | The military has been bad for most African nations because it often overthrows an elected government. |
| 2.040 | A one party government does not allow an official who is corrupt or bad at his job to be voted out of office. |

## SECTION 3

| | |
|---|---|
| 3.1 | Missionary/explorer |
| 3.2 | The Cape of Good Hope |
| 3.3 | Southern Plateau |
| 3.4 | Stone house; Shona |
| 3.5 | Namib and Kalahari |
| 3.6 | Agriculture; tea, coffee, sugar, tobacco |
| 3.7 | With Soviet paid Cuban troops |
| 3.8 | Zambezi River |
| 3.9 | War for control of the government |
| 3.10 | Natural vanilla and cloves |
| 3.11 | mouse lemur |
| 3.12 | United States and China |
| 3.13 | He was voted out of office |
| 3.14 | Zambia |
| 3.15 | Ten years |
| 3.16 | Mozambique |
| 3.17 | Madagascar |
| 3.18 | Namibia |
| 3.19 | South Africa |
| 3.20 | African kingdoms that asked for protection from white settlers who wanted their land |
| 3.21 | The white citizens |
| 3.22 | South Africa seized Namibia and held it until 1990 |
| 3.23 | The Soviet Union |
| 3.24 | Nelson Mandela |
| 3.25 | Apartheid |
| 3.26 | A working democracy |
| 3.27 | Cecil Rhodes' British South Africa Company |
| 3.28 | Chromium, gold, nickel, asbestos, copper, iron, and coal |
| 3.29 | South Africa |

# SELF TEST 3

| | |
|---|---|
| **3.01** | Nile |
| **3.02** | Kilimanjaro |
| **3.03** | Sahara |
| **3.04** | Atlas |
| **3.05** | Suez |
| **3.06** | Victoria |
| **3.07** | Volta |
| **3.08** | Tanganyika |
| **3.09** | Namib |
| **3.010** | Congo |
| **3.011** | c |
| **3.012** | f |
| **3.013** | g |
| **3.014** | e |
| **3.015** | d |
| **3.016** | a |
| **3.017** | j |
| **3.018** | h |
| **3.019** | b |
| **3.020** | i |
| **3.021** | South Africa |
| **3.022** | Madagascar |
| **3.023** | Zimbabwe |
| **3.024** | Angola |
| **3.025** | Namibia |
| **3.026** | Berlin Conference |
| **3.027** | Black president |
| **3.028** | Apartheid |
| **3.029** | Dr. David Livingstone |
| **3.030** | Government |
| **3.031** | Trade |
| **3.032** | Great Trek |
| **3.033** | Madagascar |
| **3.034** | Second |
| **3.035** | Swaziland |
| **3.036** | c |
| **3.037** | b |
| **3.038** | a |
| **3.039** | c |
| **3.040** | b |
| **3.041** | a |
| **3.042** | b |
| **3.043** | a |
| **3.044** | c |
| **3.045** | b |

# LIFEPAC TEST

| | |
|---|---|
| **l.** | Victoria |
| **2.** | Kalahari |
| **3.** | Madagascar |
| **4.** | Zambezi |
| **5.** | Indian |
| **6.** | Mediterranean |
| **7.** | Sahara |
| **8.** | Great Rift |
| **9.** | Tanganyika |
| **10.** | Nile |
| **11.** | f |
| **12.** | j |
| **13.** | i |
| **14.** | b |
| **15.** | c |
| **16.** | a |
| **17.** | e |
| **18.** | g |
| **19.** | h |
| **20.** | d |
| **21.** | Cape Verde |
| **22.** | Berlin Conference |
| **23.** | war |
| **24.** | bad (corrupt, unstable) government |
| **25.** | second |
| **26.** | one party |
| **27.** | apartheid |
| **28.** | slaves |
| **29.** | Islam, Traditional religions, Christianity (one point each answer) |
| **30.** | Sahel |
| **31.** | c |
| **32.** | a |
| **33.** | c |
| **34.** | b |
| **35.** | c |
| **36.** | a |
| **37.** | b |
| **38.** | b |
| **39.** | a |
| **40.** | b |
| **41.** | a |
| **42.** | a |
| **43.** | c |
| **44.** | c |
| **45.** | b |

# ALTERNATE LIFEPAC TEST

1. true
2. true
3. false
4. false
5. false
6. true
7. true
8. true
9. false
10. true
11. Muslims
12. Portuguese
13. Nobel Prize
14. Sudan
15. Mali, Niger, and Chad
16. independent
17. military or one party
18. rain forest/jungle
19. Liberia
20. Great Britain
21. d
22. h
23. f
24. i
25. l
26. c

27. b
28. e
29. j
30. a
31. c. Morocco
32. b. Berlin Conference
33. b. tribalism
34. c. Egypt
35. a. Suez Canal
36. c. Tanzania
37. a. Sahara
38. b. culture
39. a. discovery of oil
40. b. South Africa
41. Atlantic Ocean
42. slaves
43. sea coast
44. bad government
45. Examples:
    Libya, Tunisia, etc.
46. a. Christianity
    b. Islam
    c. Traditional
47. Examples:
    a. Liberia
    b. Sierre Leone, etc.

# HISTORY & GEOGRAPHY 607

## ALTERNATE LIFEPAC TEST

**NAME** _____

**DATE** _____

**SCORE** _____

80 / 100

**Answer true or false** (each answer, 2 points).

1. _____ David Livingstone was a missionary in Africa.

2. _____ The Nile River flows through Egypt.

3. _____ Africa varies little in its land and climate.

4. _____ The countries of Africa have been free since the late 1500s.

5. _____ Europeans have never had much interest in Africa.

6. _____ Most famines in Africa are caused by wars.

7. _____ Ghana was an empire that grew wealthy by controlling trade in gold and salt.

8. _____ Nomads were people who roamed about looking for food.

9. _____ The Equator passes just north of Africa.

10. _____ The Cape of Good Hope is on Africa's southwest corner.

**Write the correct answer from the list on each line** (each answer, 2 points).

| | | |
|---|---|---|
| Christians | Liberia | Portuguese |
| Egypt, Libya, and Tunisia | Sudan | Mali, Niger, and Chad |
| Great Britain | Muslims | rain forests/jungles |
| independent | Nobel Prize | military or one party |

11. Arabs vary in their religions, but for the most part they are _____ .

12. The first modern Europeans to contact Africa were the _____ .

13. For their peace efforts the leaders of Egypt and Israel in 1978 won the _____ .

14. The Dafur is a region in west _____ .

15. These countries are landlocked nations of the southern Sahara:

    _____ .

16. Today the African countries are mostly _____ .

17. In learning to rule themselves, many free African countries had _____

    governments.

18. Because the climate is hot and humid, Central Africa has vast _____ .

19. One country founded for freed slaves was _____ .

20. _____ held a large number of colonies in Africa at the end of World War II.

**Match these items** (each answer, 2 points).

21. _____ Congo River Basin             a. savanna

22. _____ continued lack of rain        b. Nigeria

23. _____ cereal crop                   c. Sahel

24. _____ person who flees for safety   d. Zaire

25. _____ no government or law          e. Great Rift Valley

26. _____ southern edge of the Sahara   f. millet

27. _____ Biafran War                   g. phosphate

28. _____ runs from Red Sea to          h. drought
            Mozambique
                                           i. refugee
29. _____ only African nation that did not
            become a European colony       j. Ethiopia

30. _____ tropical grasslands           k. South Africa

                                           l. anarchy

**Write the correct letter and answer on each line** (each answer, 2 points).

31. The Atlas Mountains run through _____ .
    a. Zaire                  b. Senegal              c. Morocco

32. In 1885 the European nations divided Africa up among themselves at the _____ .
    a. Casablanca Convention    b. Berlin Conference      c. Nile Treaty

33. The single greatest obstacle to African unity is _____ .
    a. disease                b. tribalism            c. ignorance

34. Anwar Sadat was the president of _____ .
    a. South Africa            b. Libya                    c. Egypt

35. Ships can go from the Mediterranean to the Red Sea using the _____ .
    a. Suez Canal              b. Nile River               c. Zaire River

36. Mt. Kilimanjaro is located in _____ .
    a. Malawi                  b. Namibia                  c. Tanzania

37. Africa's largest desert is the _____ .
    a. Sahara                  b. Namib                    c. Kalahari

38. The way of life for a people group is their _____ .
    a. economy                 b. culture                  c. religion

39. The event that has done most to change the life style of the Arabs in Libya and

    elsewhere is the _____ .
    a. discovery of oil        b. coming of missionaries   c  space age

40. Apartheid was, until the late 1980s, the official policy of _____ .
    a. Ethiopia                b. South Africa             c. Ghana

**Write the correct word on each line** (each answer, 3 points).

41. The body of water west of Africa is the _____ .

42. The first important "trade good" between Africa and Europe was _____ .

43. Landlocked countries like Mali have no _____ .

44. Many African nations are poor in spite of rich resources because of _____ .

45. Name an African nation that borders on the Mediterranean Sea. _____

**Complete these activites** (each answer, 1 point).

46. List the three major religions of Africa

    a. _____

    b. _____

    c. _____

47. Name two countries along Africa's central west coast.

    a. _____

    b. _____

# HISTORY & GEOGRAPHY 608

Unit 8: Modern Western Europe

# TEACHING NOTES

| MATERIALS NEEDED FOR LIFEPAC | |
| --- | --- |
| Required | Suggested |
| (None) | • atlas<br>• dictionary<br>• encyclopedia<br>• maps of Europe - including geography, vegetation, industries, and so forth<br>• political maps of Europe<br>• (the reference materials can be either in book or online formats) |

## ADDITIONAL LEARNING ACTIVITIES

### Section 1: The Renaissance

1. Give each student a copy of the map entitled "Countries of Western Europe." It is located in the Student Worksheets section for this unit.

2. Hand out activity sheet entitled "Western Europe—THE SOUTHERN REGION."

3. Point out to the students the countries in the southern part of Western Europe: Portugal, Spain, Italy, and Greece. Trace for them how the Renaissance grew from Italy, drawing from classical Greece and Rome, and then traveled northward.

4. Hand out activity sheet entitled "Western Europe—THE CENTRAL REGION": West Germany, the Lowland countries of Belgium and Netherlands, Switzerland, Austria, and France. Point out further the path of the spread of the Renaissance to Germany, the Netherlands, and so on.

5. Visit a local art museum or show students some good prints of Renaissance art. Ask them to discuss the art and what they like or do not like about it. Ask them why certain art pieces have become famous.

6. Discuss with the student the significance of the Martin Luther Reformation movement as well as the work of other reformers. Be sure that student realizes the reformers were part of a widespread movement of that time.

7. Ask a speaker to talk to the class. Note these suggestions: (a) an architect who can point out buildings in your city that were influenced by the Renaissance period; (b) an elected official who could trace the growth of democracy; (c) someone from Greece who can talk about the "classics," such as old buildings, and so forth.

8. Make a display of famous art, pictures of paintings, sculpture, etchings, and so forth.

9. Make a display of pictures of famous Renaissance explorers.

10. Make a display of the pictures and the work of famous Renaissance scientists.

11. With a large piece of construction paper (or other material), make a folder to hold the activities for this LIFEPAC. Title the folder "Western Europe." Also place in it the "Countries of Western Europe" map.

12. Do the activities suggested on the activity sheet entitled "Western Europe—THE SOUTHERN REGION." When you are finished, place this sheet in your folder.

13. If you wish, make a picture of the flags of the countries of southwestern Europe. Either put these flags on a piece of paper you can keep in your folder or display them on a poster.

14. Do the activities sheet entitled "Western Europe—THE CENTRAL REGION." When finished, place in your folder.

15. Add pictures of flags of central Western European countries to your flag display.

16. Make a chart or list of Protestant denominations in your city. Try to find out about the origin of each church--who founded it and where. Several are mentioned in your LIFEPAC. If you call the office of a church, someone there will probably give you information about its history.

**Section 2: The Industrial Revolution**

1. Go over Map 2 with the student. Use any other maps you have available to give the student as full a picture of the British Isles as possible. Point out that the British Isles include England, Scotland, Wales, North Ireland, and the Irish Republic.

2. Invite a local weaver or fiber hobbyist to explain to the students how people used to prepare fibers for spinning, how they spun, and how weaving is done. Sometimes there are weaving clubs in a city. (Sometimes these speakers show students pictures of spinning and weaving as it was done primitively. Then show pictures of mass production textile making. Most encyclopedias have pictures.) Discuss with the students the value of hand-crafted items.

3. Exhibit to the students pictures showing simple steam engines. (*World Book Encyclopedia* has an excellent example, and there are others.) Discuss with children the reason why the discovery of steam for engines was important at the time of the Industrial Revolution. Discuss other sources of power, such as electricity.

4. With another student, make a cardboard model of a factory city in England during the Industrial Revolution. You will have to read in encyclopedias, other books, or online about these cities. In your model be sure to include the factory and the narrow streets with two-or three-story buildings on each side. You may also want to depict the soot and coal dust covering everything.

5. Read "The Christmas Carol" by Charles Dickens to one or more classmates. This story is set in London, England, and it tells about England in the time of the Industrial Revolution. Discuss the story with each other, then between you make a list of things you learned about England from this story.

6. Color the British Isles on your activity map green. Be sure to review carefully the work you did on Map 2.

7. Test the power of steam by putting heat under your teakettle, full of water, at home. (You may do this activity in school only if your teacher says you may.) At home, get the consent of your parents. Let the water boil. Be sure to leave the lid on the teakettle. Does the steam come out of the spout in a gentle manner? It probably does at first, but when the water gets hotter, what happens to the steam? Can you guess from this experiment how mighty engines could be run by steam? If your teakettle has a whistle on the spout when does it start to whistle? What makes it whistle? What happens to the whistle when the water gets hotter?

8. Put a piece of cotton (such as a cotton ball which you have loosened or a swatch of absorbent cotton from your medicine chest at home) into the end of some tweezers. Or simply hold it between your thumb and finger tightly. As you turn the cotton, pull on it slightly.

What happens after a few minutes? You should form a yarn-like thread. You may have to try several times. Do not pull the cotton too abruptly, and turn it as fast as you can. It works better if the cotton is held with tweezers, then you can turn the tweezers more quickly. Do this experiment at school and show your teacher or a fellow student. You may want to show your parents at home. The basic idea of the spindle can be seen. Some people learn to use it so well that they can make thread as fine as spider webs. If you prefer, you may visit a workshop and find out how to use a spindle, then come back and tell the class about it.

9. If you are making a display of flags, make them for all the countries of the British Isles.

### Section 3: The Age of Unrest

1. Go over maps of Scandinavia with the students. Point out the proximity of Iceland, Greenland, and the northern coasts of North America. Point out that Scandinavia was involved in the World Wars.

2. Hand out activity sheet entitled "Scandinavia." Check to make sure that student has done his handout map well.

3. Discuss with the students the following material on the early European civilizations.

## » EARLY EUROPEAN CIVILIZATION

**European residents of today have as their ancestors many people of early civilizations.** Two of those civilization were the Celts and the Vikings.

CELTS: **The Celts spread across central and southern Europe and the British Isles.** The Celts' power lasted from about 800 B.C. to A.D. 300. The different tribes never joined in a common government. However, their common cultures still influence Western Europe. They were famous for their work with metals. Most Celts were destroyed by the Roman Empire. They were pushed over to the British Isles. Languages today of the Scots, Irish, Welsh, and some French provinces are derived from Celtics dialects. Celts also inhabited Scandinavia where they were called Nordics. The Nordics differed somewhat in physical appearance and in ways of civilization from other Celts.

VIKINGS: **The Vikings were warriors in Scandinavia a thousand years ago.** Their descendants are the Norwegians, Swedes, and Danes (natives of Denmark) of today. The Viking ships had oars as well as sails. Often it took as many as sixty oarsmen to move one boat through the icy waters of the north. Prows were always high, curved, and carved with a figure of a dragon or other being. The warlike Vikings spread out all over Europe during the eighth to the tenth centuries A.D. They had well organized systems of local government. They lived simply, even their chieftains. Their houses were made of logs with dirt floors. One famous Viking was Leif Erikson. In the year 999 he sailed the coast of Newfoundland in North America. He may have come as far south as Cape Cod, Massachusetts. Leif went back to his home in Greenland and told others about his discoveries. Some Vikings came over to settle in the new land. After a short while Indians drove them off. No Viking descendants survived in North America.

4. Go over the events of the two World Wars, with the accompanying attempts at League of Nations and the United Nations. The division of Germany and the division of Berlin may be confusing to the students. Be sure each understands the present-day condition of Germany and Berlin.

5. Write a skit about a family divided by the Berlin wall or a family trying to travel from West Germany to West Berlin on the highway that ran through the Berlin corridor. Then act out the skit with classmates.

6. Get a classmate to help you research World War I. Use encyclopedias or other references. Set up trenches or draw them of the opposing sides. These trenches had a definite plan of construction. What kind of wire divided the opposing trenches?

7. With a classmate look up the stories of several cities in Europe that were badly damaged by the blitzkriegs of World War II. Tell each other, perhaps the entire class, what you read.

8. Make a list of people you believe you could pray for in Europe. Put beside the name the reasons you wish to pray for them.

9. Complete the activity sheet entitled "Scandinavia." When you have finished this map study, put it in your folder.

10. Make a picture or model of a Viking ship.

11. If you are making a display of European flags, add the flags of the four countries of Scandinavia.

12. Find a picture in an old magazine or newspaper of Dwight D. Eisenhower. Mount the picture on a piece of paper and add it to your folder. Entitle the picture, "Head of the Allied Combined Chiefs of Staff of World War II."

# STUDENT WORKSHEETS

Included in this handbook are handouts and maps that may be reproduced on early European civilizations, Central-Western Europe, Southwestern Europe, and Scandinavia. An Answer Key for the three handout activities is provided.

## » ANSWER KEY

| COUNTRY | GOVERNMENT | LANGUAGES |
|---|---|---|
| Portugal | constitutional government | Portuguese |
| Spain | constitutional monarchy | Spanish |
| Italy | republic | Italian |
| Greece | parlimentary democracy | modern Greek |
| France | republic | French |
| Germany | federal replublic | German |
| The Netherlands | parlimentary democracy constitutional monarchy | Dutch |
| Belgium | constitutional and parlimentary monarchy | French, Dutch, German |
| Switzerland | Swiss Confederation; a federal union | German, French, Italian, Romansh |
| Austria | federal democratic republic | German |
| England | constitutional monarchy | English |
| Wales | under Great Britain | Welsh |
| Scotland | under Great Britain | Scottish |
| North Ireland | under Great Britain | Irish |
| Norway | constitutional monarchy | Norwegiam |
| Sweden | constitutional monarchy | Swedish |
| Denmark | constitutional monarchy | Danish |
| Finland | parlimentary republic | Finnish and Swedish |

# » WESTERN EUROPE — THE SOUTHERN REGION

To do this activity, you will need the activities map entitled "Countries of Western Europe." You will also need an atlas or a large map of Europe. Map 3 in your LIFEPAC will help you.

1.  On your activities map, color the countries of the Southern region blue. These will be the countries of Portugal, Spain, Italy, and Greece. Label these countries and their capitals.

2.  Place here the type of government and language of each country.

| | **Government** | **Language** |
|---|---|---|
| Portugal | _____ | _____ |
| Spain | _____ | _____ |
| Italy | _____ | _____ |
| Greece | _____ | _____ |

3.  On your map find and label the following items:

| | | |
|---|---|---|
| Iberian Peninsula | Island of Crete | Adriatic Sea |
| Island of Sardinia | Bay of Biscay | Aegean Sea |
| Island of Sicily | Mediterranean Sea | Pyrenees Mountains |
| Island of Malta | Strait of Gibraltar | Apennine Mountains |

You will not have room to label all of these, but try as many as possible.

4.  There are many very small countries. Mark these with numbers:
    1. Monaco (by France)
    2. Andorra (in the Pyrenees)
    3. San Marion (Italian Peninsula)
    4. The Vatican (Rome)

## » WESTERN EUROPE — THE CENTRAL REGION

To do this activity, you will need the activities map entitled "Countries of Western Europe." You will also need an atlas or a large map of Europe and an encyclopedia. Map 3 in your LIFEPAC will help you.

1. On your activities map, color the countries of the central region yellow. Use colored pencils and color only heavily enough for the region to be recognized. The central region consists of France, Germany, the Netherlands, Belgium, Switzerland, and Austria. Put in the capitals and label the countries.

2. Place here the type of today's government and language of each country.

|  | Government | Language |
|---|---|---|
| France | _____ | _____ |
| Germany | _____ | _____ |
| The Netherlands | _____ | _____ |
| Belgium | _____ | _____ |
| Switzerland | _____ | _____ |
| Austria | _____ | _____ |

4. On your map find and label the following items:

| The Alps Mountains | Plain of France | Seine River |
|---|---|---|
| The Pyrenees | North German Plain | Danube River |
| Brittany | Rhine River | Island of Corsica |

5. Mark these two small countries with numbers:

   1. Luxembourg (Along with the Netherlands and Belgium, it makes up area in Europe called the Lowlands.)

   2. Liechtenstein (by Germany, S, SW)

## » WESTERN EUROPE — SCANDINAVIA

To do this activity, you will need the activities map entitled "Countries of Western Europe." You will also need an atlas or a large map of Europe and an encyclopedia. Map 3 in your LIFEPAC will help you.

1.  On your activities map, color the countries of Scandinavia light lavender. Use a colored pencil. Scandinavia consists of the countries of Sweden, Denmark, Norway, and Finland. Place and label the capitals of each country and label the country.

2.  Place here the type of government and language of each country.

|         | **Government** | **Language** |
|---------|----------------|--------------|
| Norway  | _____ | _____ |
| Sweden  | _____ | _____ |
| Denmark | _____ | _____ |
| Finland | _____ | _____ |

3.  Find the following items and label them on your activities map where you have room.

| | |
|---|---|
| Jutland Peninsula | North Sea |
| Scandinavian Peninsula | Baltic Sea |
| *Artic Circle | Gulf of Bothnia |
| Barents Sea | Gulf of Finland |
| Norwegian Sea | Kjolen Mountains |
| Lake area of Finland | Lakes of Sweden |

*Draw in the Arctic Circle

Countries of WESTERN EUROPE

Atlantic Ocean

North Sea

Eastern Europe

Mediterranean

Turkey

Africa

# ANSWER KEYS

## SECTION 1

**1.1** false
**1.2** true
**1.3** false
**1.4** false
**1.5** true
**1.6** true
**1.7** Any order:
   a. learning
   b. arts
   c. architecture
   d. exploration
   e. religion
   f. science
   Also:
   Brisk trading with other countries, Italy becomes rich, Roman Catholic Church loses supremacy, strong national feelings grew, boundaries of countries defined.
**1.8** a spirit of wanting to be free
**1.9** classics or classical
**1.10** person who studies God
**1.11** eighty-nine
**1.12** sixty-seven
**1.13** dates
**1.14** older
**1.15** twenty-three
**1.16** Dürer died before El Greco was born.
**1.17** eight
**1.18** Leonardo da Vinci
**1.19** false
**1.20** true
**1.21** false
**1.22** false
**1.23** true
**1.24** false
**1.25** Example:
   The main purpose of the Renaissance explorers was to find westerly trade routes by water to India and the Far East.
**1.26** Example:
   Columbus thought the world was round. If he was right, he could get to the Far East by sailing west.
**1.27** Example:
   Vasco da Gama sailed around the southern end of Africa and into the Indian Ocean.
**1.28** Example:
   The fleet of Magellan was the first to sail around the world.

**1.29** a. reform
   b. revival
   c. remain
**1.30** a. unnecessary
   b. denomination
   c. demand
   d. awake
**1.31** became
**1.32** forgiveness
**1.33** a. include
   b. important
   c. individual
**1.34** h
**1.35** f
**1.36** i
**1.37** c
**1.38** g
**1.39** e
**1.40** b
**1.41** d
**1.42** the scientific method
**1.43** the telescope
**1.44** Sparta and Athens
**1.45** King John
**1.46** Either order:
   a. How to fly like a bat
   b. How to float on water
**1.47** Examples:
   Learning did more to influence life in the United States because it led to the kind of schools we now have; arts and architecture showed that men's minds were free to create beauty and to express thoughts of the common man; exploration has opened new doors and encouraged new findings; science became important because our lives are better because of scientific knowledge; government prepared to now live in a democracy; inventions created many conveniences for the modern world.
**1.48** Italy
**1.49** Germany
**1.50** England
**1.51** Italy
**1.52** Switzerland
**1.53** Scotland
**1.54** Netherlands or Holland
**1.55** Italy

## SELF TEST 1

| | | | | |
|---|---|---|---|---|
| **1.01** | false | | **1.025** | b |
| **1.02** | false | | **1.026** | h |
| **1.03** | true | | **1.027** | e |
| **1.04** | true | | **1.028** | j |
| **1.05** | true | | **1.029** | a |
| **1.06** | false | | **1.030** | i |
| **1.07** | true | | **1.031** | Greeks and Romans |
| **1.08** | false | | **1.032** | feudal manors |
| **1.09** | true | | **1.033** | Medici Bank |
| **1.010** | false | | **1.034** | the merchants who built them |

**1.011**  a.  religious subject
**1.012**  c.  The Last Supper
**1.013**  a.  the life of the people
**1.014**  a.  painter and sculptor
**1.015**  c.  make men feel the love of God close to
              them
**1.016**  a.  Spain
**1.017**  b.  Renaissance Period
**1.018**  d.  San Salvador Island
**1.019**  b.  first to go around the world
**1.020**  c.  Cabral
**1.021**  k
**1.022**  f
**1.023**  d
**1.024**  c

**1.035**  telescope
**1.036**  strong national feelings
**1.037**  all trustworthy scientists
**1.038**  Magna Carta (or Great Charter)
**1.039**  Greece
**1.040**  Gutenberg
**1.041**  Any order:
              a.  exploration
              b.  science
              c.  government or religion, invention, art,
                  architecture, learning
**1.042**  Example:
          By faith in Jesus Christ he accepts God's gift
          of salvation.

# SECTION 2

**2.1** false
**2.2** true
**2.3** false
**2.4** true
**2.5** false
**2.6** true
**2.7** true
**2.8** true
**2.9** true
**2.10** false
**2.11** a. charcoal
b. factories
**2.12** Either order:
a. rivers
b. streams
**2.13** a. furnaces
b. iron
**2.14** a. soot
b. coal
**2.15** black country
**2.16** James Watt
**2.17** convenient
**2.18** a. Eli Whitney
b. United States
**2.19** cotton
**2.20** a. locomotives
b. ships
**2.21** England
**2.22** textiles
**2.23** Any order:
a. the spinning jenny could spin hundreds of threads on separate spindles at one time
b. the roller spinning frame spooled all of these threads at one time
c. the flying shuttle carried the wool through the warp quickly
**2.24** Either order:
a. roads
b. waterways (canals)
**2.25** Rural life disappeared.
Prople crowded the cities.

**2.26** men, women, and children
**2.27** started Sunday schools
**2.28** Example:
Because of John Wesley's teaching, many Christians became aware of bad conditions and took steps to improve them.
**2.29** Any three of these answers:

Because of growth in population in home countries and in new colonies, more people needed to be supplied with goods, which led to increased demand for products. Also the colonies supplied new raw materials for manufacture making extra industry possible.

New inventions led to greater manufacturing efficiencies, such as steam engine, spinning jenny, roller frame, flying shuttle, cotton gin. New kinds of power, such as coal, steam, and later electricity made the new inventions workable. Also, factories could be moved to convenient locations.

or

Improved transportation methods such as steam locomotives, steamships, and better canals, carried products to consumers further and faster.

**2.30** Teacher check
**2.31** England
**2.32** England
**2.33** c
**2.34** a
**2.35** e
**2.36** b
**2.37** d
**2.38** f

# SELF TEST 2

| | |
|---|---|
| 2.01 | d |
| 2.02 | b |
| 2.03 | g |
| 2.04 | i |
| 2.05 | e |
| 2.06 | c |
| 2.07 | a |
| 2.08 | k |
| 2.09 | h |
| 2.010 | j |
| 2.011 | c. Canada |
| 2.012 | b. invention |
| 2.013 | a. coal |
| 2.014 | b. steam engine |
| 2.015 | c. United States |
| 2.016 | d. mechanical engineer |
| 2.017 | b. widened and deepened canals |
| 2.018 | a. natural resources |
| 2.019 | c. priest |
| 2.020 | a. Lippershey |
| 2.021 | Leonardo da Vinci |
| 2.022 | Petrarch |
| 2.023 | crowded |
| 2.024 | 1492 |
| 2.025 | faith in Christ alone |
| 2.026 | an architect |
| 2.027 | England |
| 2.028 | Brazil |
| 2.029 | Reformed |
| 2.030 | spindle |
| 2.031 | false |
| 2.032 | true |
| 2.033 | true |
| 2.034 | true |
| 2.035 | true |
| 2.036 | false |
| 2.037 | false |
| 2.038 | true |
| 2.039 | false |
| 2.040 | true |

2.041 Any Order:
   a. the spinning jenny could spin hundreds of threads on separate spindles at one time
   b. the roller spinning frame spooled all of these threads at once
   c. the powered flying shuttle carried the woof through the warp quickly

2.042 Any order:
England had enough natural resources. England's navy could back up her trade routes. England's colonies were reasonably stable.

# SECTION 3

3.1 Either order:
   a. its northern province of Alsace-Lorraine from Germany
   b. settlement of dispute with Germany over Morocco

3.2 two provinces with seaport from Austria-Hungary

3.3 Any order:
   a. colonies for new products and resources
   b. colonies in which to invest money
   c. bases where they could put military supplies and men

| | |
|---|---|
| 3.4 | false |
| 3.5 | false |
| 3.6 | true |
| 3.7 | true |
| 3.8 | false |
| 3.9 | false |
| 3.10 | true |
| 3.11 | false |
| 3.12 | false |
| 3.13 | true |
| 3.14 | true |
| 3.15 | true |
| 3.16 | Teacher check |

3.17 Any order:
   a. Germany
   b. Italy
   c. Hungary
   d. Romania
   e. Bulgaria
   f. Finland

3.18 Any four of these answers:
   a. blitzkrieg
   b. strategy
   c. espionage
   d. extermination or psychological underground

3.19 Any three of these answers:
   a. bitterness over Versailles Treaty
   b. Germany's loss of faith and hope
   c. rise of dictatorships
   or economic depression League of Nation's failure

3.20 Any order:
   a. Russia-Stalin, Lenin, Communism
   b. Mussolini, Italy, Fascist
   c. Nazi, Germany, Hitler

**3.21** Any order:
a. Denmark
b. Norway
c. Belgium
d. France

**3.22** Any order:
a. France
b. Great Britain
c. United States
d. Russia

**3.23** Any order:
a. China
b. United States
c. Russia
d. Great Britain

**3.24** Example:
The people of Berlin were divided from the other side of their city. Their country is divided. Many people could not see their families or friends for years. Communism failed and the Berlin wall was destroyed.

**3.25** Example:
I would not be able to go to my grandmother's house. I would not be able to attend my favorite ball games. We could not go to the church my family has attended for years. I could not play with my friend.

**3.26** Any order:
a. Germany
b. Italy
c. Hungary
d. Russia
e. Romania
f. Bulgaria
g. Finland
h. Japan

**3.27** Any order:
a. Great Britain
b. France
c. United States
d. China
e. Russia

**3.28** Teacher check

# SELF TEST 3

**3.01** c. a seaport
**3.02** a. secret diplomacy
**3.03** b. 1914
**3.04** b. League of Nations
**3.05** a. German Nazis
**3.06** a. 1939
**3.07** b. General Eisenhower
**3.08** a. air blitzes and strategy
**3.09** c. the murder of Archduke Ferdinand
**3.010** c. United Nations
**3.011** depression
**3.012** Berlin or Germany
**3.013** lowered
**3.014** Great Britain
**3.015** hymns
**3.016** coal
**3.017** natural
**3.018** learning
**3.019** rebirth, renewal, or revival
**3.020** the classics
**3.021** d
**3.022** f
**3.023** i
**3.024** a
**3.025** k
**3.026** c
**3.027** e
**3.028** g
**3.029** j
**3.030** h
**3.031** Either answer:
national socialism or Nazism
**3.032** Fascism
**3.033** communism
**3.034** They were all dictators.
**3.035** Example:
A dictator is a person who tells everyone else what to do. In countries it is the head of government who runs all of the government by himself.
**3.036** Example:
The city itself was divided between free Germany and the Russian section. Berlin was separated from the rest of West Germany.
**3.037** Example:
spinning thread and weaving
**3.038** Example:
By faith in Jesus Christ alone he comes to God.

# LIFEPAC TEST

1. renewal or rebirth or revival
2. Magna Carta
3. lightning war
4. classics
5. Ferdinand
6. spindle
7. Martin Luther
8. Magellan's
9. Hitler
10. inventions
11. c
12. e
13. h
14. j
15. b
16. a
17. k
18. f
19. d
20. i
21. b. gave the people a voice in the government
22. b. Johann Gutenberg
23. c. take out the seeds
24. c. weave the thread
25. b. coal
26. a. the scientific method
27. b. on farms
28. b. Petrarch
29. a. Russia
30. a. Nazi Party
31. true
32. true
33. true
34. false
35. false
36. true
37. true
38. true
39. true
40. false
41. Either order; Examples:
    a. Boundaries had been drawn to please the ruling monarchs and these sometimes caused disputes.
    b. Countries were in competition for colonies.
    Also acceptable:
    The immediate reason was the killing of Archduke Ferdinand.
42. Example:
    By faith in Jesus he comes to God.

# ALTERNATE LIFEPAC TEST

1. d. a wall
2. c. short and sickly
3. c. religion
4. d. went around the world
5. a. life of the people
6. c. pulls and spools the thread
7. d. Martin Luther
8. b. Hitler
9. c. an inventor
10. a. textile manufacture
11. i
12. g
13. e
14. j
15. d
16. b
17. f
18. k
19. c
20. a
21. Communism
22. Fascism
23. blitzkrieg
24. trenches
25. hymns
26. spinning
27. market
28. resources
29. weaving
30. school
31. Example:
    Berlin was divided by the Soviets from part of its mother country. Because of the Berlin wall, it was divided within itself. (Both points must be made.)
32. Example:
    A Christian can approach God directly.
33. true
34. true
35. true
36. false
37. false
38. false
39. true
40. true
41. false
42. false

# HISTORY & GEOGRAPHY 608

## ALTERNATE LIFEPAC TEST

**NAME** _____

**DATE** _____

**SCORE** _____

**Write the correct letter and answer on each line** (each answer, 2 points).

1. In Berlin before 1989 the east side of the city was divided from the west by _____ .
   a. railroad tracks      b. cable cars          c. a white line          d. a wall

2. John Wesley was _____ .
   a. strong and healthy                    b. an athlete
   c. short and sickly                      d. young when he died

3. Art in the Middle Ages was all about _____ .
   a. icons              b. children          c. religion              d. still life

4. One of Magellan's ships _____ .
   a. was a rowboat                         b. shipwrecked in Tierra
   c. turned back to Spain                  d. went around the world

5. Renaissance artists began to depict _____ .
   a. life of the people                    b. landscapes
   c. church life only                      d. city life

6. The spinning frame _____ .
   a. has warp and woof threads             b. spins thread
   c. pulls and spools the thread           d. was used to darn socks

7. The Protestant Reformation was started by _____ .
   a. John Knox                             b. the Huguenots
   c. John Wesley                           d. Martin Luther

8. *Mein Kampf* was written by _____ .
   a. Marx              b. Hitler          c. Mussolini          d. Stalin

9. Lippershey was primarily _____ .
   a. a teacher         b. a sailor         c. an inventor         d. Stalin

10. England's major industry during the Industrial Revolution was _____ .
    a. textile         b. mining         c. navigation         d. inventing

**Match these items** (each answer, 2 points).

| | | | |
|---|---|---|---|
| 11. | _____ Cabral | a. | ninety-five theses |
| 12. | _____ Petrarch | b. | painter and sculptor |
| 13. | _____ Magna Carta | c. | British Isles |
| 14. | _____ Columbus | d. | printing press |
| 15. | _____ Gutenberg | e. | Runnymede, England |
| 16. | _____ Michelangelo | f. | early Greek writings |
| 17. | _____ classical | g. | man can reason for himself |
| 18. | _____ suffix | h. | central Europe |
| 19. | _____ North Ireland | i. | discovered Brazil |
| 20. | _____ Martin Luther | j. | 1492 |
| | | k. | after a word |

**Write the correct answer on the line** (each answer, 3 points).

21. The political belief of Lenin was _____ .

22. Mussolini's political belief was _____ .

23. One important method of combat in World War II using air power was the _____ .

24. World War I was mostly fought on the ground in _____ .

25. Charles Wesley was the writer of great _____ .

26. The machine invented during the Industrial Revolution that makes many strands of thread or yarn at one time is called the _____ jenny.

27. The economic depression of the 1930s was brought on by the failure in 1929 of the stock _____ .

28. England became leader of the Industrial Revolution partly because it had an abundance of natural _____ .

29. The flying shuttle is used in cloth _____ .

30. During the Industrial Revolution, Robert Raikes started the Sunday _____ .

**Answer these questions** (each answer, 5 points).

31. What was the Berlin tragedy? _____

_____

_____

_____

32. How can a Christian approach God? _____

_____

_____

_____

**Write true or false** (each answer, 2 points).

33. _____ During the Industrial Revolution, the population of Western Europe grew steadily.

34. _____ The manufacture of iron products needed coal for fuel.

35. _____ England's filthy cities during the Industrial Revolution caused the passage of the Public Health Act.

36. _____ Mussolini was head of the Italian Communists.

37. _____ If you wish to pray, you must ask your minister to pray for you.

38. _____ Martin Luther lived during the Industrial Revolution.

39. _____ World War II started when Germany marched on Poland.

40. _____ Many people still migrate from the Communist side to West Berlin.

41. _____ Steam power was rejected by manufacturers as being no good.

42. _____ Factory owners during the Industrial Revolution gave special favors to their child laborers.

# HISTORY & GEOGRAPHY 609

Unit 9: Modern Eastern Europe

# TEACHING NOTES

| MATERIALS NEEDED FOR LIFEPAC | |
|---|---|
| Required | Suggested |
| (None) | • dictionary<br>• encyclopedias<br>• maps of Eastern Europe<br>• (the reference materials can be either in book or online formats) |

## ADDITIONAL LEARNING ACTIVITIES

**Section 1: Government and Churches of Early Eastern Europe.**

1. Using as many maps as are available to you, go over with the students various significant facts about the early Byzantine world.

   a. Location of Constantinople, Greece, Italy (especially Rome), Asia Minor, the Holy Land, and Egypt as well as other parts of Africa.

   b. Note the water access from Constantinople to the world through the Bosporus, the Sea of Marmara, the Aegean Sea, and the Mediterranean Sea; also to Russia via the Black Sea. Trace the easy water route from Kiev, Russia, down the Dnieper River, over the Black Sea to Constantinople.

2. Show student an interior view of St. Sophia's Orthodox Church (or other). Try to define the squares of columns from which the domes arise. Half domes rise from two columns (or half squares).

3. Help student with mosaic if grout is used (see Independent Activities).

4. Display pictures of illuminated manuscripts. Discuss with student. Notice the amount of gold paint used. Why are they called *illuminated*?

5. Take a large piece of modeling clay. Lay it flat and smooth on your desk or other surface. Trace a design on the top of it (which you have made very smooth.) You will probably want to do this activity with another student. Now take a flat tool, like a paring knife, and dig gently around the outside of your design. Your design should include a border around the edge. Do not dig into the design itself or into the border. When you have finished, so that only your design and the border remain on the original surface, you will have a *bas-relief*. Display in the classroom.

6. Take a piece of poster cardboard about 20" by 15" (or whatever size you need). Fold the cardboard so you have two sides 10" by 15". Now, paste two religious pictures on each side of the inside fold. Now you have something similar to a diptych, except that most diptyches have a hinge in the middle. If you wish, you could glue a narrow stick to the back and carry it above you as you walk around the room. Many diptyches are carried in Orthodox Church solemn parades. How would the pictures you used differ from the pictures on a diptych of the early Orthodox Church? Reread the information on Church Art in your LIFEPAC.

7. Some encyclopedias and books have details of the city of ancient Constantinople. Make a model, or a picture diagram, of this city and show it to the class. Constantinople. Make a model, or a picture diagram, of this city and show it to the class.

8. Take a heavy piece of cardboard or a piece of wood and trace a design on it. Then take small pieces of colored tile or glass and fill in your design. You do this by putting glue on the portion of the design you wish to fill with a certain color. Put that color tile or glass on the glue. Fill the entire design in this manner, one color at a time. You now have a mosaic. However, to make it more authentic and to hold your tile in more securely, you should pour grout between the tile. Let your teacher or a parent help you. Look at pictures of mosaics to get a better idea of how to accomplish this activity.

9. If you started a display of European flags for Western Europe (LIFEPAC 608), you may now add to it the flag of ancient Constantinople. The reading on Constantine 1 discusses the use of *standards* in the empire. Look up the word *standard* in a dictionary if you do not know its meaning.

10. Copy, by tracing, the Chi Rho cross from your LIFEPAC. Transfer to a piece of plastic, such as the lid of a margarine container of coffee can. Cut out around the outlines. Put a hole in the very top of the R. Run a string, ribbon, or chain through it for a neck piece or a bracelet.

## Section 2: Countries of Eastern Europe, Early History

1. Locate the current countries in the former country of Yugoslavia.

2. Talk extensively with the student about the modern physical maps of Eastern Europe. Point out that the Ural Mountains make a natural dividing point between European Russia and Asian Russia. In Romania show how Transylvania is cut off from the other two provinces by the Carpathian Mountains and the Transylvanian Alps. Show as many types of maps, such as industries, crops and so forth as possible.

3. Make sure the student understands why Greece was more closely related to the Western world than to Eastern Europe in our time.

4. Impress on the student how long six hundred years is--much longer than the United States has been a nation. The Turks occupied the Balkans for almost this long yet the countries managed to keep some of their cultures and heritages intact.

5. Choose either a Slav village or a castle. Make a model of it. This activity will require research. Put together all the facts you learned about either a Slav village or a castle, show your model, and give a collective report to your class.

6. Research the national costumes of several of the countries of Eastern Europe. Most people in these countries today dress like we do in the United States for every day. For festivals and other special occasions, however, they wear the clothes of their forefathers and call them costumes (even as we do in colonial costumes). If you have enough helpers, you could pretend to have your own festival, or you could show the class pictures of the costumes. Tell the class what you have learned about the dress of the countries.

7. Pull apart a cotton ball, or get some absorbent cotton from a package and make three very thin pads of cotton about 1" by 2". Under your teacher's supervision (or parent's), put one pad of the cotton on a heavy mat or ironing board. Heat an iron to high heat. Then wet the cotton pad with a water spray until it is saturated. Put a wet paper towel over it and press the hot iron down hard on top. When it is dry from the heat, remove the paper towel over it and put another pad on top of the first cotton pad while it is still hot. Saturate both with water and recover with a wet paper towel. Iron until dry and repeat with the third cotton pad. How many cotton pads do you now have? If your heat was right and you pressed hard, you should have only one, and the pad you now have should be reasonably hard to pull apart. You have made a bit of felt with cotton fiber. Look at a piece of commercial felt. It

is pressed under scientific conditions with cotton fibers, too. The felt of the early-history years were made of fibers of animal hair, goat, sheep, and so forth. People made this fabric before spinning and weaving.

8. If you have a display of European flags, add those of Russia, Poland, the Czech Republic, Slovakia, Hungary, Germany, Romania, Bulgaria, Albania, Slovenia, Croatia, Bosnia & Herzegovina, Macedonia, Serbia, and Kosovo.

9. List the names of the capitals of each country on a sheet of paper or a display card. Beside each capital name one outstanding characteristic of this city. You may add more than one characteristic if you wish to. You will have to read at least one outside reference to complete this activity.

10. Ask your teacher if you may make a display on the bulletin board of pictures you can cut from old magazines about life in these countries.

## Section 3: Countries of Eastern Europe, Modern History

1. Have the students trace the Arctic Circle. How close is it to the North Pole? What is the weather like? Consider the duration of sunlight and the seasons.

2. Make a list of comparisons between the life of a boy or girl in the United States and one in a Communist country. Then write and act out a skit that will depict these differences.

3. Make a list of people or conditions in the former communist nations of Europe that you would like to pray for. Show your list to your teacher.

4. Read some resource material on the space program in Russia. Also read about adventures in space in the United States. Make a poster showing the various advances both programs have made.

5. During the period of time you are working on this LIFEPAC, study your newspapers for news items about any of the countries or people of Eastern Europe. Cut out the items and bring the clippings to school. Perhaps you could paste them to a poster or display them on the bulletin board.

6. Look up information on the *aurora borealis*. What is another name for it? Tell a classmate and your teacher what you found out.

7. Discuss the events of 1989 and the fall of communism in Europe. The students should give their own ideas about why it happened.

8. Compare a map of Europe before 1989 with a map in 1995. Draw or trace a map of the new countries that were created out of communist Yugoslavia. Discuss how the war there has changed the map.

# ANSWER KEYS

## SECTION 1

**1.1**   false
**1.2**   true
**1.3**   false
**1.4**   false
**1.5**   true
**1.6**   true
**1.7**   false
**1.8**   false
**1.9**   false
**1.10**  true
**1.11**  a.  Constantinople
         b.  Black
         c.  Marmara
         d.  Mediterranean
         e.  Aegean
         f.  Golden Horn
         g.  Rome
         h.  impregnable
         i.  Bosporus
         Examples:
         Constantine made Constantinople the capital
         instead of Rome. Its harbor was the Golden
         Horn and it was impregnable.
         The Bosporus strait connects the Black sea
         to the Sea of Marmara, which flows into the
         Aegean and
         Mediterranean.
**1.12**  Examples:
         Byzantia was closer to Greece.
         Rome was cut off from Constantinople.
**1.13**  Justinian
**1.14**  Turks
**1.15**  prosperity
**1.16**  crusaders
**1.17**  Constantinople
**1.18**  true
**1.19**  true
**1.20**  false
**1.21**  false
**1.22**  true

**1.23**  false
**1.24**  false
**1.25**  true
**1.26**  false
**1.27**  true
**1.28**  j
**1.29**  c
**1.30**  h
**1.31**  b
**1.32**  d
**1.33**  e
**1.34**  f
**1.35**  a
**1.36**  g
**1.37**  false
**1.38**  true
**1.39**  false
**1.40-1.49**  Examples:
**1.40**  a.  to fall down
         b.  a season of the year
**1.41**  a.  he fell down
         b.  a harsh blow (He felled the tree.)
**1.42**  a.  to possess
         b.  to acknowledge, admit
**1.43**  a.  a disposition
         b.  a crucifying device
**1.44**  a.  ability to act
         b.  math-to the power
**1.45**  a.  to give portions
         b.  business arrangement
**1.46**  a.  a political division (State of Nevada)
         b.  a condition of mind or to tell a fact
**1.47**  a.  to defend, a reserve for animals
         b.  keep from decay (pickle)
**1.48**  a.  first, original
         b.  put in working order
**1.49**  a.  strictly accurate
         b.  to assess—to compel to be paid (to exact
             a fee)

# SELF TEST 1

**1.01** from Rome to Constantinople

**1.02** Istanbul

**1.03** Example:
a vision of a cross, plus the fact they won the battle and the Empire

**1.04** Bosporus

**1.05** barbarians from the north

**1.06** Roman

**1.07** Justinian

**1.08** burned it down or sacked it

**1.09** c

**1.010** j

**1.011** f

**1.012** b

**1.013** i

**1.014** e

**1.015** a

**1.016** d

**1.017** g

**1.018** h

**1.019** Examples:
The church structure was different and the church services were different. Their architecture featured domes. Their art could never show how people really looked. Paintings were flat sculptures bas-relief. Their contact with the world was limited. They were in touch with the Turks and Muslims. They were nearer the Middle East and the Holy Land.

**1.020** b. Turkey

**1.021** a. a golden age

**1.022** d. centralized

**1.023** c. fragmented

**1.024** b. Chi Rho

**1.025** a. Marmara and Aegean seas

**1.026** c. Vladimir

**1.027** b. 300s

**1.028** d. 500s

**1.029** a. code of Roman laws

**1.030** a. It begins east of Greece, on the Bosporus, Black Sea, Sea of Marmara, Aegean Sea. At one time it spread all around the Mediterranean.
b. Constantinople

**1.031** a. Constantine
b. Justinian

**1.032** Eastern Orthodox Church

**1.033** Either order:
a. icons, bas-relief, lacy carvings, diptych, silk fabrics
b. domes, illuminated manuscripts, manuscripts, mosaics

**1.034** Examples:
He saw a vision and defeated his enemies. or He named Constantinople.
He moved the capital of the Empire from Rome to Constantinople. He moved the emperors to Constantinople. He made Constantinople impregnable.

**1.035** Examples:
a. He built the church of St. Sophia.
b. He coded the Roman laws. or He brought the Roman Empire partly back together. He spoke Latin, and kept the empire together.

# SECTION 2

| | | | |
|---|---|---|---|
| **2.1** | Teacher check | **2.26** | Teacher check |
| **2.2** | true | **2.27** | true |
| **2.3** | false | **2.28** | false |
| **2.4** | true | **2.29** | true |
| **2.5** | false | **2.30** | false |
| **2.6** | true | **2.31** | false |
| **2.7** | families | **2.32** | a. Turkey |
| **2.8** | pit houses | **2.33** | c. Transylvania |
| **2.9** | Moscow | **2.34** | c. trickery |
| **2.10** | St. Petersburg | **2.35** | b. 1877 |
| **2.11** | c. dogs | **2.36** | public baths |
| **2.12** | a. army | **2.37** | Danube River |
| **2.13** | c. 126 years | **2.38** | Bulgars |
| **2.14** | a. American Revolution | **2.39** | Cyrillic |
| **2.15** | c. World War II | **2.40** | Teacher check |

**2.16** b

**2.17** d

**2.18** h

**2.19** g

**2.20** a

**2.21** i

**2.22** e

**2.23** f

**2.24** Example:
Wilhelm II was emperor of Germany from 1888 to 1918. He had many troubles, but under him the country did well, especially in the south. Food was plentiful. Mines, mills, manufacturing, even science, prospered.

**2.25** Example:
Germans (or Teutons) have been in the area of Germany since before Christ. However, the country of Germany did not form until Bismark united the little Germanies late in the 19th century. The country prospered until World War I. Germany became a republic after the war, but started World War II over dispute of the Peace Treaty of World War I. Germany was divided into East and West after World War II.

**2.41** Example:
The Balkans had more Turkish influence. They were occupied by the Turks longer. Islam religion is prominent. They had no Renaissance and were related to the Byzantine world. They relate to Greece hardly at all.

**2.42** i

**2.43** d

**2.44** h

**2.45** g

**2.46** c

**2.47** b

**2.48** f

**2.49** a

**2.50** true

**2.51** true

**2.52** false

**2.53** true

**2.54** true

**2.55** true

**2.56** true

# SELF TEST 2

| | |
|---|---|
| **2.01** | e |
| **2.02** | j |
| **2.03** | d |
| **2.04** | i |
| **2.05** | k |
| **2.06** | h |
| **2.07** | b |
| **2.08** | g |
| **2.09** | a |
| **2.010** | f |
| **2.011** | Czech Republic |
| **2.012** | Moscow |
| **2.013** | Hungary |
| **2.014** | Bucharest |
| **2.015** | Berlin |
| **2.016** | Bulgaria |
| **2.017** | Poland |
| **2.018** | Belgrade |
| **2.019** | Tirane |
| **2.020** | Constantinople |
| **2.021** | a. moved from place to place |
| **2.022** | c. families |
| **2.023** | b. domes |
| **2.024** | d. black robes |
| **2.025** | c. codes of law |
| **2.026** | b. flaming cross |
| **2.027** | a. six people's republics |
| **2.028** | c. 500 years |
| **2.029** | a. Magyar |
| **2.030** | d. Poland |
| **2.031** | Cyrillic |
| **2.032** | Kiev |
| **2.033** | Turks |
| **2.034** | Slavs |
| **2.035** | The Czech Republic and Slovakia. |
| **2.036** | shipbuilding |
| **2.037** | Dnieper |
| **2.038** | <u>bas-relief</u> |
| **2.039** | trickery |
| **2.040** | Bulgars |

# SECTION 3

| | |
|---|---|
| **3.1** | false |
| **3.2** | false |
| **3.3** | true |
| **3.4** | true |
| **3.5** | true |
| **3.6** | true |
| **3.7** | false |
| **3.8** | true |
| **3.9** | false |
| **3.10** | goals |
| **3.11** | business or enterprise |
| **3.12** | classless |
| **3.13** | State |
| **3.14** | Example:<br>Representative Democracies have more than one candidate to vote on in an election. In communist countries, people vote on a chosen candidate. Our laws are made by Congress, not by the Politburo. Everything belongs to the State in a communist country; in a representative democracy, anyone can start a business and earn a profit. Local governments in communism are under the rule of the central government. In a representative democracy, states are expected to rule themselves. Laws in communism help the state; in a representative democracy they aid the people. |
| **3.15** | a. One is free to worship.<br>b. The government will restrict churches. |
| **3.16** | a. The government really cares.<br>b. The government wants to look good to the world. |
| **3.17** | a. These are Russia's lawmakers.<br>b. They pass laws made by the Politburo. |
| **3.18** | a. People have a voice in government.<br>b. People elect those chosen by Politburo. |
| **3.19** | a. One is free to speak or write.<br>b. Many writers and others have been jailed or detained |
| **3.20** | a. Communism offers plenty to people.<br>b. Communism will take all and give nothing. |
| **3.21** | East Germany and West Germany |
| **3.22** | Solidarity |
| **3.23** | Velvet Revolution |
| **3.24** | Berlin Wall |
| **3.25** | Hungarian |
| **3.26** | Lech Walesa |
| **3.27** | 74 |

**3.28** a. Yugoslavia
   b. Macedonia
   c. Croatia
   d. Slovenia
   e. Bosnia & Herzegovina
**3.29** Albania and Yugoslavia
**3.30** Nicolae Ceausescu
**3.31** Albania
**3.32** a. Serbs
   b. Croats
   c. Muslims
**3.33** Bulgaria
**3.34** force or military force
**3.35** Teacher check

# SELF TEST 3

**3.01-3.03** Examples:

**3.01** The Slavs lived in pit houses half dug into the ground (with tunnels connecting them). The village was made up of members of a clan or an extended family. When the soil in one place was not fit for planting the clan moved and set up a village elsewhere, but they'd come back to the original village in a few years.

**3.02** Communism is run by the state. Everybody serves the state. In a democratic republic, people live for themselves. In communism, only one candidate runs for office. The candidate is chosen by those who run the government. In a democratic republic, laws are made by Congress, not the Politburo. In communism, no one can own a business.

**3.03** A democratic republic is planned to give the people the most freedom and happiness possible. The laws and government are meant to make life for the citizens as good as possible. In communism, people do not count except to promote the government and the country.

**3.04** e
**3.05** c
**3.06** a
**3.07** j
**3.08** d
**3.09** i
**3.010** k
**3.011** h
**3.012** f
**3.013** b
**3.014** property or business
**3.015** military force
**3.016** Politburo
**3.017** unrest or dissension
**3.018** Lenin
**3.019** dome
**3.020** Justinian
**3.021** Prague
**3.022** Russia
**3.023** Albania
**3.024** a. Moscow
**3.025** b. East Berlin
**3.026** a. Romania
**3.027** c. public baths
**3.028** d. Bosporus
**3.029** b. Mikhail Gorbachev
**3.030** b. Yugoslavia
**3.031** c. cruel

**3.032** c. Bolsheviks
**3.033** a. reducing the Secret Police
**3.034** stones or tiles
**3.035** Bulgaria
**3.036** capitalism
**3.037** parties
**3.038** Solidarity

# LIFEPAC TEST

| | |
|---|---|
| I. | false |
| 2. | true |
| 3. | true |
| 4. | false |
| 5. | true |
| 6. | true |
| 7. | false |
| 8. | true |
| 9. | false |
| 10. | true |
| 11. | Balkan peninsula |
| 12. | Dual Monarchy |
| 13. | Constantine |
| 14. | icons |
| 15. | Romans |
| 16. | Orthodox |
| 17. | bishop |
| 18. | mosaic |
| 19. | bas-relief |
| 20. | Transylvania |
| 21. | c |
| 22. | b |
| 23. | b |
| 24. | c |
| 25. | c |
| 26. | b |
| 27. | c |
| 28. | Moscow, Russia |
| 29. | Budapest, Hungary |
| 30. | Prague, Czech Republic |
| 31. | Warsaw, Poland |
| 32. | Berlin, Germany |
| 33. | Sofia, Bulgaria |
| 34. | Belgrade, Yugoslavia |
| 35. | Tirane, Albania |
| 36. | Bucharest, Romania |

28–32. North and Central
33–36. Balkan

# ALTERNATE LIFEPAC TEST

1. five year plans
2. silk
3. Danube
4. Tito
5. checks and balances
6. Orthodox Christ Child
7. Islam
8. Peter the Great
9. black robes
10. Communism
11. false
12. true
13. false
14. true
15. true
16. true
17. false
18. true
19. true
20. false

21-29 Any order:
21. Moscow, Russia
22. Budapest, Hungary
23. Berlin, Germany
24. Prague, Czech Republic
25. Warsaw, Poland
26. Tirane, Albania
27. Belgrade, Yugoslavia
28. Bucharest, Romania
29. Sofia, Bulgaria
30. d. secret ballot
31. b. the state
32. d. Slovakia
33. b. Lenin
34. c. Chi Rho
35. d. Slavs
36. a. Vladimir

# HISTORY & GEOGRAPHY 609

## ALTERNATE LIFEPAC TEST

**NAME** _____

**DATE** _____

**SCORE** _____

80

100

**Write the correct word from the list on each line** (each answer, 3 points).

| | | |
|---|---|---|
| black robes | five-year plans | silk |
| checks and balances | Islam | Tito |
| communism | Orthodox Christ Child | wool |
| Danube | Peter the Great | |

1.  Stalin of the USSR thought up the idea of the _____ .

2.  Byzantine fabrics were often made of _____ .

3.  The river that divides Bulgaria from Romania is the _____ .

4.  The first communist leader of Yugoslavia was _____ .

5.  The United States President, Congress, and the Supreme Court have a system of

    _____ .

6.  A man's face is on every _____ .

7.  The Turkish religion is _____ .

8.  Workingmen's clothes were put on by _____ .

9.  Eastern Orthodox priests and monks always wear _____ .

10. Revolution is a tool of _____ .

**Answer true or false** (each answer, 2 points).

11. _____ In a representative democracy the people serve the state.

12. _____ The Slavs lived in clans of extended families.

13. _____ In communism everyone owns his own house.

14. _____ Communism collapsed in Europe in 1989.

15. _____ The Turks finally conquered the Byzantine Empire.

16. _____ The sculpture of ancient Byzantium was mostly bas-relief.

17. _____ Constantine saw a vision of a riderless horse.

18. _____ Mikhail Gorbachev began the reforms in the USSR that ended the Cold War.

19. _____ The Turks occupied the Balkan Peninsula for five hundred years.

20. _____ In communism the state serves the people.


**Place the capital with its correct country** (each answer, 4 points).

<u>Capitals</u>

21. _____ , _____ Belgrade

22. _____ , _____ Berlin

23. _____ , _____ Bucharest

24. _____ , _____ Budapest

25. _____ , _____ Moscow

26. _____ , _____ Prague

27. _____ , _____ Sofia

28. _____ , _____ Tirane

29. _____ , _____ Warsaw


**Write the correct letter and answer on the line** (each answer, 2 points).

30. In a representative democracy, elections are held by _____ .
  a. king's edict                          b. selected voters
  c. force                                 d. secret ballot

31. In communism everything is controlled by _____ .
  a. the weather        b. the state        c. the people        d. Congress

32. The country that did not exist before 1989 was _____ .
  a. Poland             b. Bulgaria          c. East Germany       d. Slovakia

**33.**  Hungry people in Russia, around World War I, were promised food by _____ .
a.  Karl Marx          b.  Lenin              c.  Stalin              d.  Khrushchev

**34.**  The name of Constantine's cross is _____ .
a.  crucifixion        b.  Maltese            c.  Chi Rio            d.  German

**35.**  The people who settled most of Eastern Europe were the _____ .
a.  Celts              b.  Vikings            c.  Greeks             d.  Slavs

**35.**  The name of the Russian prince who brought the Orthodox Church to his country was

_____ .

a.  Vladimir           b.  Romanov           c.  Peter              d.  Podgorny

# HISTORY & GEOGRAPHY 610

Unit 10: Development of Our World

# TEACHING NOTES

| MATERIALS NEEDED FOR LIFEPAC | |
|---|---|
| **Required** | **Suggested** |
| • encyclopedias<br>• overhead or opaque projector<br>• dictionary<br>• large pieces of paper or cloth<br>• construction paper<br>• marking pens<br>• atlas and globe<br>• poster board<br>• paste, scissors<br>• clay or newspapers for paper-mâché<br>• old magazines for pictures | • Books: *Afanasev's Russian Fairy Tales*<br>      *Life in the Middle Ages*<br>      *African Tribal Customs*<br><br>• (the reference materials can be either in book or online formats) |

## ADDITIONAL LEARNING ACTIVITIES

**Section 1: Cradle of Civilization.**

1. Review map study of Mesopotamia, Israel, and Egypt. Be sure the student knows the exact areas of the Fertile Crescent. Would a person living in China or India consider this location to be the "Cradle of Civilization"?

2. Invite a Jewish person to speak to the class about the role of children in family Jewish celebrations. Take the class to a Bar or Bat Mitzvah.

3. Do some research; then, with another student, try making a model of a shaduf. Explain to other students or the classroom how water was lifted this way.

4. Study Egypt's hieroglyphics. Read the book, Hieroglyphics for Fun by Henry Joseph Scott. Try making your own secret hieroglyphic code. Make up messages to pass back and forth to each other.

5. If you were Jewish, when you are thirteen years old, you would become responsible for your own sins and religious behavior. Your family could give you a great party after you have conducted a service in the synagogue. Pretend you are having your Bar or Bat Mitzvah (Bath or Bas Mitzvah for a girl) under the supervision of your Rabbi. Prepare a talk such as the one you would give. Choose a portion of the Torah you would read to the congregation. Present to your classroom or Sunday school class.

**Section 2: Greece, Rome, and the Middle Ages**

1. Go over with students the meaning of the words "classics from the Greeks and Romans," especially Greek. These classics came to be the basis of the "awakenings" of the Renaissance.

2. Review the reasons for the Dark Ages and Middle Ages: barbarians were not as advanced or educated as the Romans, fierce competition between kings and lords, the feudal system,

very little schooling, and plagues. Discuss these with students, plus other reasons that may have contributed to this era.

3. Look in books on the Middle Ages or search online and find games children played during that period. Ask a librarian to help you. How many of these games resemble games you play today? Either plan a game session using Middle Ages games for your classmates, or make a display with drawings or pictures. Entitle it "Children's Games in the Middle Ages."

## Section 3: Modern Nations of Europe

1. Review with the student these points about Western Europe:

   a. the Renaissance, remembering specific areas, and including the Protestant Reformation;

   b. the good and bad points of the Industrial Revolution;

   c. the two World Wars; why they were fought and the difference in methods of warfare;

   d. the divisions of Germany and Berlin; and

   e. the League of Nations and the United Nations.

2. Review with the student these points about Eastern Europe:

   a. The Orthodox Church

   b. communism in Russia and its major leaders;

   c. communism in all Eastern Europe;

   d. difference between communist and democratic thought; and

   e. the fall of communism in Europe.

3. On the wall of your room at school, hang a large piece of paper or cloth about the size of a bed sheet. Anchor the bottom and top with long strips of wood so that it can be rolled up or down for storage.  With an opaque or an overhead projector, enlarge a map of all of Europe onto the paper or cloth. Take marking pens and copy the map while it is projected. When you have finished copying, fill in the names of each country, the capitals of each country, and the major rivers and mountains of each area. You may add anything else you wish.

4. Find a book of Russian fairy tales and read some of them. Remember that the fairy tales that we have known came mostly from Western Europe. How do the fairy tales of Russia differ from the ones we know? Are they longer or shorter? Are the characters and situations any different? Write a report or give an oral report to the class about the difference between Eastern and Western European fairy tales.

## Section 4: South America and Africa

1. Review the names of the countries of South America, both northern and southern. Go over the physical map of South America with the student, locating the high Andes, the low jungles and chaco areas, the cooler southcentral, and the rocky bleak south. Discuss any topics the student may have found difficult.

2. Review Africa with the student, the countries of the north, central, and southern parts. Go over as many political problems of Africa as seem important and necessary. If students choose to do a large wall map of Africa, they will probably need help with the many countries.

3.  Make large wall maps of South America and of Africa. For each you will need a large piece of paper or cloth, about the size of half a bed sheet. Use an opaque or overhead projector. Be sure to put in all the countries, their capitals, and the major mountains and rivers of each area. Do one map at a time. Anchor with wood strips.

4.  Look up in references:

    a.  the artifacts of the ancient Inca civilization or

    b.  works of African art.

    Try to copy some of them. Use clay, salt clay, or papier-mâché. When they are dry, paint them. Display them on a shelf in your classroom, being careful to label the country and artifact each represents.

5.  Go back over the South American LIFEPACS (605, 606). Write down all the crafts and hand-work done today by people in various parts of South America. Make a chart or poster of these crafts, such as weaving by the Otavalo Indians in Ecuador. Illustrate with drawings or pictures if possible.

6.  Make masks such as those worn in tribal ceremonies in Africa. Do research in books and then tell the class what the mask or masks you made represent.

7.  Read some folk tales of Africa and tell them over to a classmate or the class.

## STUDENT WORKSHEET

A handout sheet is provided that may be reproduced for the students. They may use the illustrations to identify Greek and Roman columns. No answer key is needed.

# GREEK AND ROMAN COLUMNS

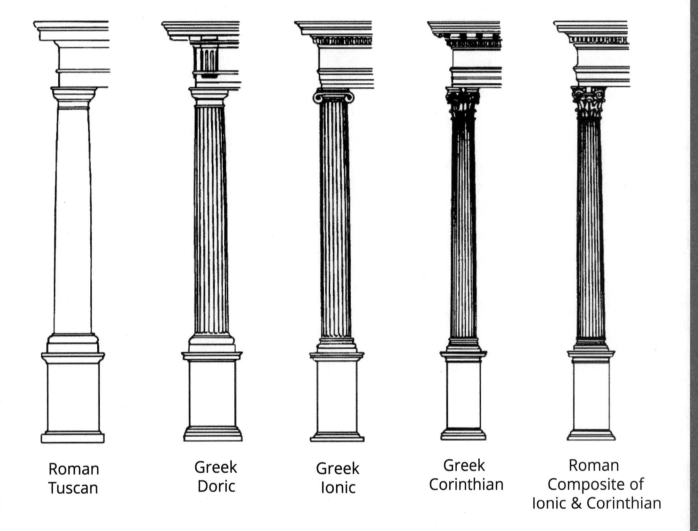

Roman
Tuscan

Greek
Doric

Greek
Ionic

Greek
Corinthian

Roman
Composite of
Ionic & Corinthian

# ANSWER KEYS

## SECTION 1

| | |
|---|---|
| **1.1** | c |
| **1.2** | d |
| **1.3** | a |
| **1.4** | g |
| **1.5** | i |
| **1.6** | b |
| **1.7** | h |
| **1.8** | f |
| **1.9** | true |
| **1.10** | true |
| **1.11** | false |
| **1.12** | true |
| **1.13** | false |
| **1.14** | true |
| **1.15** | Any order: |

a. written language
b. multiplication and division
c. wheel
d. plow with metal tip
e. shaduf or good roads, weaving of cloth, weights and measures

| | |
|---|---|
| **1.16** | Africa |
| **1.17** | Nile River |
| **1.18** | Pharaoh |
| **1.19** | pyramids |
| **1.20** | architecture |
| **1.21** | stone |
| **1.22** | laborers |
| **1.23** | outside world |
| **1.24** | Examples: |

a. No
b. The Egyptians who worshiped one god still worshiped a god of their own creation and not the one true God.

| | |
|---|---|
| **1.25** | a |
| **1.26** | b |
| **1.27** | a |
| **1.28** | c |
| **1.29** | b |
| **1.30** | c |

## SELF TEST 1

| | |
|---|---|
| **1.01** | true |
| **1.02** | false |
| **1.03** | true |
| **1.04** | true |
| **1.05** | false |
| **1.06** | true |
| **1.07** | true |
| **1.08** | false |
| **1.09** | true |
| **1.010** | true |
| **1.011** | b |
| **1.012** | a |
| **1.013** | c |
| **1.014** | b |
| **1.015** | a |
| **1.016** | b |
| **1.017** | c |
| **1.018** | c |
| **1.019** | c |
| **1.020** | a |
| **1.021** | kings |
| **1.022** | Nile River |
| **1.023** | Mediterranean Sea |
| **1.024** | stones |
| **1.025** | laborers |
| **1.026** | cloth |
| **1.027** | language |
| **1.028** | many gods |
| **1.029** | metal tip |
| **1.030** | many gods |
| **1.031** | d |
| **1.032** | h |
| **1.033** | k |
| **1.034** | f |
| **1.035** | i |
| **1.036** | c |
| **1.037** | e |
| **1.038** | j |
| **1.039** | b |
| **1.040** | g |
| **1.041** | Example: |

It was in this region where more than one early civilization began and later spread to other areas.

| | |
|---|---|
| **1.042** | Example: |

The Hebrew people worshiped the one true God. The people of Mesopotamia and Egypt worshiped many different gods of their own creation.

# SECTION 2

| | |
|---|---|
| **2.1** | b |
| **2.2** | a |
| **2.3** | c |
| **2.4** | b |
| **2.5** | c |
| **2.6** | b |
| **2.7** | c |
| **2.8** | Example: |

The Peloponnesian War weakened the empire of Greece. City-states began to fight among themselves. The fighting made it easier for Greece to be conquered.

**2.9** Any order:
a. worshiped many gods
b. spoke same language
c. had same literature
or celebrated Olympic Games

| | |
|---|---|
| **2.10** | buildings |
| **2.11** | columns |
| **2.12** | geometry |
| **2.13** | latitude and longitude |
| **2.14** | mathematics |
| **2.15** | Hippocratic oath |
| **2.16** | instruments |
| **2.17** | by jury |
| **2.18** | Greek |
| **2.19** | Roman Empire |
| **2.20** | false |
| **2.21** | true |
| **2.22** | true |
| **2.23** | true |
| **2.24** | false |
| **2.25** | true |
| **2.26** | true |
| **2.27** | false |
| **2.28** | false |
| **2.29** | true |
| **2.30** | false |
| **2.31** | true |

**2.32**
a. Rome is located on the peninsula of Italy.
b. After gaining control of Italy, Rome fought the Punic Wars.
c. Unrest existed in Rome for a while.
d. A triumvirate was a government by three persons.
e. Augustus Caesar was the first Roman emperor.

| | |
|---|---|
| **2.33** | d |
| **2.34** | g |
| **2.35** | j |
| **2.36** | a |
| **2.37** | c |
| **2.38** | f |
| **2.39** | b |
| **2.40** | i |
| **2.41** | h |

**2.42** Any order:
a. dishonesty
b. violence
c. decrease in trade
d. decrease in value of money
e. laws which took away people's freedom to choose jobs or overworked soil, poor crop harvests

**2.43** Dark Ages and Middle Ages

**2.44** Example:
Each king had a kingdom and lived in a castle. Each king also had a group of loyal nobles who fought for him. He gave land to each noble. This land was called a manor. Each noble lived in a castle. Each noble gave land to vassals. Vassals were required to perform certain duties for the noble. Each manor had its own village. A villein was a person who was required to work for the noble every day. A villein lived in his own house in the village. A serf was a slave and belonged to the noble.

**2.45** Teacher check

**2.46** Example:
Part of the Middle Ages was called the Dark Ages because most schools and books had been destroyed. It was a dark period because many wars were fought, education was at a standstill, and health and sanitation practices were primitive.

**2.47** a. garbage
b. disease
c. water

**2.48** x

**2.49** does not describe

**2.50** x

**2.51** x

**2.52** x

**2.53** does not describe

**2.54** x

**2.55** does not describe

**2.56** x

**2.57** true

**2.58** false

**2.59** true

**2.60** true

**2.61** true

**2.62** true

**2.63** false

**2.64** true

**2.65** Any order:
a. Crusades
b. interest in learning
c. prosperity of merchants and townspeople

## SELF TEST 2

**2.01** true
**2.02** true
**2.03** true
**2.04** false
**2.05** true
**2.06** false
**2.07** true
**2.08** true
**2.09** true
**2.010** false
**2.011** a
**2.012** c
**2.013** a
**2.014** a
**2.015** a
**2.016** c
**2.017** b
**2.018** c
**2.019** a
**2.020** c
**2.021** manor
**2.022** castles
**2.023** village
**2.024** slave
**2.025** garbage
**2.026** books or the Bible
**2.027** Catholic Church
**2.028** schools
**2.029** the one true God
**2.030** Fertile Crescent
**2.031** d
**2.032** j
**2.033** a
**2.034** g
**2.035** i
**2.036** b
**2.037** k
**2.038** h
**2.039** e
**2.040** c
**2.041** Example:
Many wars were fought. Few books and few schools were available to the people during the Dark Ages. Health and sanitation practices were primitive.
**2.042** Any order:
a. Crusades
b. interest in learning
c. prosperity of merchants and townspeople

# SECTION 3

| | |
|---|---|
| **3.1** | c |
| **3.2** | h |
| **3.3** | i |
| **3.4** | a |
| **3.5** | b |
| **3.6** | d |
| **3.7** | f |
| **3.8** | j |
| **3.9** | e |
| **3.10** | Any order: |
| | a. ask forgiveness |
| | b. receive salvation |
| | c. read the Scriptures |
| **3.11** | Example: |
| | New freedom in learning was the foundation for America's freedom of thought and religion. |
| **3.12** | Magna Carta |
| **3.13** | all people |
| **3.14** | freedom in government |
| **3.15** | equal |
| **3.16** | govern themselves |
| **3.17** | b |
| **3.18** | a |
| **3.19** | c |
| **3.20** | a |
| **3.21** | b |
| **3.22** | b |
| **3.23** | c |
| **3.24** | a |
| **3.25** | true |
| **3.26** | false |
| **3.27** | true |
| **3.28** | true |
| **3.29** | false |
| **3.30** | true |
| **3.31** | false |
| **3.32** | true |
| **3.33** | true |

| | |
|---|---|
| **3.34** | b |
| **3.35** | a |
| **3.36** | b |
| **3.37** | c |
| **3.38** | a |
| **3.39** | a |
| **3.40** | c |
| **3.41** | a |
| **3.42** | Any order: |
| | a. economic depression |
| | b. dictatorships |
| | c. political problems |
| **3.43** | Any order: |
| | a. Hitler - Germany |
| | b. Stalin - Russia |
| | c. Mussolini - Italy |
| **3.44** | Japan attacked Pearl Harbor. |
| **3.45** | Example: |
| | Germany was divided into four sections. One section was given to Russia and is known as East Germany today. One section each was given to France, Britain, and the United States. These three sections are known as West Germany today. Berlin was divided in the same way. |
| **3.46** | the United Nations |
| **3.47** | orthodox |
| **3.48** | communism |
| **3.49** | Any order: |
| | a. classless society |
| | b. all business, industry, control of money should belong to government |
| | c. state is all important or there is no God |
| **3.50** | true |
| **3.51** | false |
| **3.52** | true |
| **3.53** | true |
| **3.54** | false |
| **3.55** | false |

# SELF TEST 3

**3.01** true
**3.02** true
**3.03** false
**3.04** true
**3.05** true
**3.06** true
**3.07** true
**3.08** true
**3.09** true
**3.010** true
**3.011** b
**3.012** a
**3.013** b
**3.014** c
**3.015** a
**3.016** a
**3.017** b
**3.018** c
**3.019** b
**3.020** a
**3.021** steam
**3.022** children
**3.023** wages
**3.024** 1939
**3.025** territory or land
**3.026** size
**3.027** by jury
**3.028** city-states
**3.029** disease or plagues
**3.030** proven guilty
**3.031** i
**3.032** c
**3.033** g
**3.034** a
**3.035** k
**3.036** f
**3.037** b
**3.038** h
**3.039** d
**3.040** e
**3.041** Example:
Mikhail Gorbachev began to give the people in the USSR and Eastern Europe more freedom. The people used their new freedom to end communism.

**3.042** Example:
Communism believes that there is no God. Communism believes a person should give all of his time and energy to the state. Communism discourages involvement in religion and church. A person cannot attend church and belong to the Communist Party. Democracy gives each individual the freedom to attend church whenever and

wherever he chooses.

# SECTION 4

**4.1** Any order:
 a. Brazil, Portugal
 b. Venezuela, Spain
 c. Colombia, Spain
 d. Guyana, Great Britain
 e. Suriname, Netherlands
 f. French Guiana, France

**4.2** Any order:
 a. Indian
 b. European
 c. African

**4.3** a, c

**4.4** a, b

**4.5** b

**4.6** c

**4.7** c

**4.8** d

**4.9** Example:
Some missionaries live in villages with the Indians. Some missionaries translate the Bible into native languages. Some use radio programs to spread God's word.

**4.10** aluminum

**4.11** Spain

**4.12** Inca

**4.13** Paraguay

**4.14** hostile

**4.15** peaceful

**4.16** president

**4.17** military

**4.18** a, b

**4.19** c

**4.20** a

**4.21** c

**4.22** b

**4.23** a

**4.24** c

**4.25** a

**4.26** b

**4.27** a

**4.28** c

**4.29** c

**4.30** a

**4.31** a

**4.32** Around the few sources of water, like the Nile, or as nomads

**4.33** Peace and good government

**4.34** The end of the Cold War

**4.35** Islam

**4.36** Islamic fundamentalists

**4.37** Any order:
 a. Mauritania
 b. Algeria
 c. Libya
 d. Sudan
 e. Niger
 f. Morocco
 g. Tunisia
 h. Egypt
 i. Mali
 j. Chad
 k. Western Sahara
 l. South Sudan

**4.38**
 a. x
 b. x
 c. blank
 d. x
 e. x
 f. blank
 g. x
 h. x
 i. x
 j. blank
 k. blank
 l. x
 m. x
 n. x
 o. x
 p. x
 q. blank
 r. x
 s. x
 t. blank
 u. blank
 v. x
 w. x
 x. x
 y. x
 z. x
 aa. blank
 bb. x
 cc. x
 dd. x
 ee. x
 ff. x
 gg. x
 hh. x
 ii. x
 jj. blank

**4.39** Strong African tribes captured people from weaker tribes and sold them to the Europeans.

**4.40** Tropical rain forests surrounded by savanna.
**4.41** one party or military governments.
**4.42**  a.  Angola
  b.  Botswana
  c.  Lesotho
  d.  Madagascar
  e.  Malawi
  f.  Mozambique
  g.  Namibia
  h.  South Africa
  i.  Swaziland
  j.  Zambia
  k.  Zimbabwe
**4.43** b
**4.44** e
**4.45** a
**4.46** c
**4.47** d

# SELF TEST 4

**4.01** true
**4.02** true
**4.03** true
**4.04** true
**4.05** true
**4.06** true
**4.07** false
**4.08** false
**4.09** false
**4.010** true
**4.011** c
**4.012** b
**4.013** a
**4.014** c
**4.015** a
**4.016** b
**4.017** c
**4.018** a
**4.019** b
**4.020** a
**4.021** Islam
**4.022** Sahara Desert
**4.023**  a.  one party
  b.  military
**4.024** slaves
**4.025**  a.  peace
  b.  good government
**4.026** bauxite
**4.027** awakening or rebirth
**4.028** Middle Ages or Dark Ages
**4.029** guilds
**4.030** Crusades
**4.031** c
**4.032** f
**4.033** d
**4.034** j
**4.035** a
**4.036** i
**4.037** e
**4.038** g
**4.039** k
**4.040** h
**4.041** Example:
Vasco da Gama discovered southern Africa during his search for a water route to India. Portugal established settlements and trading posts.
**4.042** Examples:
Children had to work in factories and did not go to school. Cities became dirty and overcrowded. Some farmland was taken over by factories. Workers received small wages and worked long hours.

# LIFEPAC TEST

1. false
2. false
3. true
4. true
5. true
6. true
7. true
8. false
9. true
10. false
11. b
12. a
13. a
14. c
15. b
16. a
17. c
18. a
19. b
20. b
21. Any order:
    a. oil, petroleum
    b. coffee
    c. salt
    d. bauxite
    e. spices
    f. bananas
    g. vanadium
    or sugar, cotton, wool, tin, cattle, sheep, lumber, trucks, automobiles, tractors, jets, copper, iron, silver, coal

22. Any order:
    a. peace
    b. good government
23. d
24. k
25. e
26. j
27. a
28. i
29. f
30. b
31. c
32. g
33. Examples:
    The Fertile Crescent had sufficient water, good soil, and a warm climate. These factors influenced its growth as the Cradle of Civilization.
34. Either order a-b:
    a. many jobs available
    b. people could buy good products at low cost
    or brought new inventions, unions were formed, more products could be made in less time, trade increased
    Either order c-d:
    c. cities became dirty and overcrowded
    d. children had to work in factories and could not go to school
    or workers paid small wages and worked long hours, factories were built on farmland

# ALTERNATE LIFEPAC TEST

1.  b.  Tigris and Euphrates rivers
2.  a.  Africa
3.  c.  Israel
4.  b.  rich
5.  a.  harbors
6.  a.  apartheid
7.  c.  Magna Carta
8.  b.  children
9.  a.  metal
10. c.  crusades
11. false
12. true
13. true
14. false
15. true
16. true
17. true
18. false
19. false
20. true
21. h
22. d
23. e
24. b
25. a
26. j
27. c

28. g
29. i
30. f
31. bauxite
32. Bolivia
33. Renaissance
34. Africa
35. South America
36. slaves
37. shaduf
38. Hippocrates
39. jury
40. Revolution
41. Example:
    Germany and Berlin were divided in four parts to France, Great Britain, United States, and the Soviet Union. France, Great Britain, and the United States let the Western parts govern themselves. The USSR made her share communistic. Berlin had a high wall down the middle. This wall caused much sorrow because people could not go back and forth.
42. Answer must be student's own, but to be accepted, must show perception and good judgment.

# HISTORY & GEOGRAPHY 610

## ALTERNATE LIFEPAC TEST

**NAME** _____

**DATE** _____

**SCORE** _____

**Write the correct letter and answer on each line** (each answer, 2 points).

1.  Mesopotamia was located along the _____ .
    a. Nile River
    b. Tigris and Euphrates rivers
    c. Jordan River

2.  Egypt is located in northeastern _____ .
    a. Africa                    b. Mesopotamia                    c. Israel

3.  The Fertile Crescent covered Egypt, Mesopotamia, and _____ .
    a. Asia Minor                b. India                          c. Israel

4.  The soil of the Fertile Crescent was _____ .
    a. rocky                     b. rich                           c. sandy

5.  Greece became a trading empire because of her good, natural _____ .
    a. harbors                   b. rivers                         c. mountains

6.  The racial policy of South Africa was _____ .
    a. apartheid                 b. equality                       c. checks and balances

7.  One important document signed during the Renaissance was _____ .
    a. Declaration of Independence
    b. Articles of Confederation
    c. Magna Carta

8.  During the Industrial Revolution a great number of laborers were _____ .
    a. elderly men               b. children                       c. cripples

9.  The Mesopotamians used a plow with a tip made of _____ .
    a. metal                     b. wood                           c. stone

10. Journeys to save the Holy Land were called _____ .
    a. Holy Grail                    b. pilgrimages                    c. crusades

**Write true or false** (each answer, 2 points).

11. _____ The New Testament was first written in Latin.

12. _____ World War I began in 1914.

13. _____ The Roman Empire built many good roads.

14. _____ Stalin was a kindly president of the Soviet Union.

15. _____ Brazil produces more coffee than any other country.

16. _____ Ecuador, Peru, and Bolivia were all, at one time, controlled by Spain.

17. _____ Life in Africa is centered around the tribes.

18. _____ Most North African people are Israelites.

19. _____ Athens and Sparta were two Egyptian city-states.

20. _____ Greek architecture is known for its stately columns.

**Match these items** (each answer, 2 points).

21. _____ Five Year Plan

22. _____ Lenin, Stalin

23. _____ World War II began

24. _____ Orthodox Church

25. _____ Armistice

26. _____ United States

27. _____ Communism falls in Europe

28. _____ Hebrews

29. _____ rich soil and water

30. _____ tombs of Pharaohs

a. 1918

b. Eastern Europe Church

c. 1989

d. Communist leaders

e. 1939

f. pyramids

g. Old Testament

h. Communist Soviet Union

i. Fertile Crescent

j. Allied Power

k. spindles

**Write the correct word on the line** (each answer, 3 points).

31.   Aluminum is made from _____ .

32.   Tin is mined in _____ .

33.   Another word for *rebirth*, or *awakening*, is _____ .

34.   Cameroon is located in Central _____ .

35.   Uruguay is located in Southern _____ .

36.   Early traders to Africa were primarily looking for_____ .

37.   In Mesopotamia the device for lifting water was called the _____ .

38.   Doctors today still take the Grecian Oath of _____ .

39.   Greece introduced the concept of trial by _____ .

40.   Dirty streets and overcrowded towns became common during the Industrial

_____ .

**Answer these questions** (each answer, 5 points).

41.   Explain how Germany and Berlin came to be divided and what those divisions were. What effect did the divisions have on the people there?

_____

_____

_____

_____

42.   Which area of Level 600 Social Studies did you like best and why?

_____

_____

_____

_____